GIRL WARRIOR

ALSO BY JOY HARJO

For a Girl Becoming

Washing My Mother's Body: A Ceremony for Grief

Remember

Weaving Sundown in a Scarlet Light: Fifty Poems for Fifty Years

Catching the Light

Poet Warrior: A Memoir

Living Nations, Living Words: An Anthology (editor)

When the Light of the World Was Subdued, Our Songs Came Through: A Norton Anthology of Native Nations Poetry (editor, with LeAnne Howe, Jennifer Elise Foerster, and contributing editors)

An American Sunrise

Conflict Resolution for Holy Beings

Crazy Brave: A Memoir

Soul Talk, Song Language: Conversations with Joy Harjo (with Tanaya Winder)

For a Girl Becoming

She Had Some Horses

How We Became Human: New and Selected Poems, 1975–2001

A Map to the Next World

The Good Luck Cat

Reinventing the Enemy's Language: Contemporary Native Women's Writings of North America (editor, with Gloria Bird)

The Spiral of Memory (edited by Laura Coltelli)

The Woman Who Fell from the Sky

Fishing

In Mad Love and War

Secrets from the Center of the World
(with photographs by Stephen E. Strom)

What Moon Drove Me to This?

The Last Song

MUSIC ALBUMS

I Pray for My Enemies

Red Dreams: A Trail Beyond Tears

Winding Through the Milky Way

She Had Some Horses

Native Joy for Real

Letter from the End of the Twentieth Century

PLAYS

We Were There When Jazz Was Invented

Wings of Night Sky, Wings of Morning Light

GIRL WARRIOR

On Coming of Age

Joy Harjo

W. W. NORTON & COMPANY
Independent Publishers Since 1923

Copyright © 2025 by Joy Harjo-Sapulpa

All rights reserved
Printed in the United States of America
First Edition

For information about permission to reproduce selections from this book, write to Permissions, W. W. Norton & Company, Inc., 500 Fifth Avenue, New York, NY 10110

For information about special discounts for bulk purchases, please contact W. W. Norton Special Sales at specialsales@wwnorton.com or 800-233-4830

Manufacturing by Lakeside Book Company
Book design by Chris Welch
Production manager: Lauren Abbate

ISBN: 978-1-324-09417-3

W. W. Norton & Company, Inc.
500 Fifth Avenue, New York, NY 10110
www.wwnorton.com

W. W. Norton & Company Ltd.
15 Carlisle Street, London W1D 3BS

10 9 8 7 6 5 4 3 2 1

For the ancestors who were once young in their becoming. For the stories they pass on to us as we dream and create—

For the children, grandchildren, great-grandchildren past, present, and future—

For the young women I meet, have met, and will meet along this poetry and music road. Know that we see you. We hear you. You are beauty, strength, and accomplishment even as you struggle to become in a world that often works against your empowerment. You are made of the prayers of those before you who love you.

We believe in you.

"The humma-hah (meaning 'long ago') stories are traditional Pueblo stories that have been told continuously for thousands of years about a time when amazing things were possible, when the plants and animals and even rocks and stars used to converse with human beings. The humma-hah stories describe the various supernatural beings and other worlds and other times that still exist right beside the present world and present time."

—Leslie Marmon Silko, Laguna Pueblo novelist and poet

"In the end, we will all become stories."

—Margaret Atwood, novelist

"The secret of our success is we never give up."

—Chief Wilma Mankiller, Cherokee

Contents

For Calling the Spirit Back from Wandering the Earth in Its Human Feet

Put down that bag of potato chips, that white bread, that bottle of pop.
Turn off that cell phone, computer, and remote control.
Open the door, then close it behind you.
Take a breath offered by friendly winds.
They travel the earth gathering essences of plants to clean.
Give back with gratitude.
If you sing it will give your spirit lift to fly to the stars' ears and back.
Acknowledge this earth who has cared for you since you were a dream planting itself precisely within your parents' desire.
Let your moccasin feet take you to the encampment of the guardians who have known you before time, who will be there after time.
They sit before the fire that has been there without time.
Let the earth stabilize your postcolonial insecure jitters.
Be respectful of the small insects, birds, and animal people who accompany you.
Ask their forgiveness for the harm we humans have brought down upon them.
Don't worry.

The heart knows the way though there may be high-rises,
interstates, checkpoints, armed soldiers, massacres, wars, and those
who will despise you because they despise themselves.
The journey might take you a few hours, a day, a year, a few years, a
hundred, a thousand or even more.
Watch your mind. Without training it might run away and leave
your heart for the immense human feast set by the thieves of time.
Do not hold regrets.
When you find your way to the circle, to the fire kept burning by
the keepers of your soul, you will be welcomed.
You must clean yourself with cedar, sage, or other healing plant.
Cut the ties you have to failure and shame.
Let go the pain you are holding in your mind, your shoulders, your
heart, all the way to your feet. Let go the pain of your ancestors to
make way for those who are heading in our direction.
Ask for forgiveness.
Call upon the help of those who love you.
Call yourself back. You will find yourself caught in corners and
creases of shame, judgment, and human abuse.
You must call in a way that your spirit will want to return. Speak to
it as you would to a beloved child.
Welcome your spirit back from its wandering. It will return in
pieces, in tatters. Gather them together. They will be happy to be
found after being lost for so long.
Your spirit will need to sleep awhile after it is bathed and given
clean clothes.

Now you can have a party. Invite everyone you know who loves and supports you. Keep room for those who have no place else to go. Make a giveaway, and remember, keep the speeches short. Then, you must do this: help the next person find their way through the dark.

1 The Story Field

I was young in my poetry making. I was a mother to two young children, with a full-time job, and tending to what my art demanded. I was beset by dreams that were appearing more and more dimensional and real. I was as awake in them as I was in my living.

In one of my dreams, I was taken by a guardian far above the earth. Earth was dressed in blue and green. She was lit from within. I was enveloped in a lush darkness that extended forever to eternity. Space was not empty, rather there was a profound depth of sound presence, like an echo stacked within many layers of echoing. There were blues that don't exist in everyday earthly existence. Stars and planets glimmered like giant-colored diamonds. I was in a circle of exquisite belonging.

When I looked more closely at the detail, I saw a lit field of stories. They were all over the world, through all time. The stories were constantly shifting in shape and color. Where there was kindness there was light. Meanness made upheaval. There were those who created light and shared it, and others who stole and devoured it.

Every story that ever happened made an imprint in the field. The past was just as mobile as the present and the future. Everyone's thoughts, dreams, and actions were motivated by the story direction. The energetic particles around and through everything were made of what we Mvskoke people call *vnokeckv*, or love. It is a fierce love that is strong enough to compel to beauty and right action. It is a love beyond what is fully comprehensible by any singular mind.

It is happening now.

In the dream, I understood that we are the earth, Ekvnvcakv, or Mother Earth in my Mvskoke language; we are the story. All of this was shown to me, then I woke up. I was much like you. I turned off the alarm, slid out of bed, and stepped into the details of the day.

2 Woven

You are intrinsic to the weave of a story that is so large you will never see the beginning or ever the end of it. After I became a grandmother in my late thirties, and a great grandmother earlier than most, as I researched and gathered the stories of ancestors, of our tribal nation history, I began to see how each person is an essential part in a familial continuum.

As each child came into our family, I saw how, though family members may have passed on, they continued, in some manner or the other, through those coming up. It was in their physical features, gestures, or expressions. When I held one granddaughter, I could feel the same shape of muscular energy I had felt when I had held her mother at birth. Of course, I saw and see my daughter and myself in all her children, my grandchildren, but each is unique. Then there are the gifts. On my mother's side it was guitars, impatience, and teaching. On my father's it was painting, speaking, and bravery. Bad habits are passed along as well as the tendency to kindness. We carry a wealth of stubbornness which can also translate as resilience. Some family members even carry memories of being together in a time before.

As I studied the weave, it became apparent that the reason we call aunties and uncles our mothers and fathers, nieces and nephews our children, our cousins our brothers and sisters, is to strengthen the weave. There is a powerful over and under weave between grandparents and grandchildren, and it extends for generations. The weave makes a road for ancestors to travel, so they can visit, and pass on wisdom, stories. And some of them like to return to stir up trouble again, the way they did when they were living.

3 *Mystery*

Some things are unexplainable according to three-dimensional linear time and place. Quantum physics opens a mathematical pathway. So does ceremonial practice. You might ponder mystery with your everyday mind but you will not be able to cross over toward understanding unless you switch to dream-think, or another kind of thinking that is more intuitive. That's where poetry comes in, where math makes a path.

I was called to the Wind River Reservation in the nineteen eighties because there had been a rash of teen suicides. The outbreak was so shocking and disturbing that it made national news. The community was trying everything to stop it. The teenage years are meant for exuberance and joy, for testing the story, for becoming independent and finding yourself alongside others in your generation who are facing similar themes, the same challenges. For any of our beloved young to despair so much that they would take their lives was unthinkable, unacceptable. The Wind River community decided that poetry workshops would help the young people, with their own feelings of turmoil and despair, and with grief at the loss of their friends.

The Wind River Reservation is one of the most striking places in all my travels. A tough beauty flows through the hills, defines the rolling earth, and outlines the mountains where colored ground touches skies. I was welcomed in by the community. I found a circle of young people who were creative and lively, who were open and had plenty to say in poetry about who they were and what they were facing. Like other Native youth, they were under tremendous stress. Their reservation, like others, had high rates of poverty, violence, and addiction from historical trauma that went back several generations, since the genocidal acts of a foreign government. The students dealt daily with racism and culturalism, which are embedded in the country's educational, religious, and other social structures. Their families often lacked resources available in communities outside the reservation.

The students also had the usual challenges in the transformational time between childhood and adulthood. The teen years are like the chrysalis stage, when a caterpillar becomes a butterfly. There's so much happening inside that no one can see, and when it's happening you can't explain because you don't yet understand. There's so much innate power in that becoming yet it might not feel like power. It can feel like chaos. Your body transforms, as does your mind and your emotional field. You don't trust the advice of those who have gone through it and survived and even thrived because you don't quite trust yourself. These are the years in which you are making crucial decisions about what your path might look like as you are reforming. It is a vulnerable and very powerful time. This period of chrysalis-making can happen at any time of great transformation; it can happen for individuals, communities, nations, and countries.

The students' spirits shone in poetry. They found a way to speak when everyday language could not cross over into revelation. Many were also excellent artists.

One day they told me about a mystery. Before a suicide they would see a black sedan circle the reservation. In the car were white men wearing suits and sunglasses. The next morning another of their friends would be gone. No one knew quite what to make of it. There was no foul play in the deaths.

If I consider this in dream-think, as a poet, it occurs to me that a black sedan and its occupants represent power. Those kinds of cars are expensive. You must have money for those high-priced items like their suits and sunglasses. The occupants hiding their eyes with dark glasses are hiding their intention. They packed weapons and it is the threat and use of massive gunpower that took over control of our indigenous lands. This kind of power depends on constant patrolling of borders and citizens. The black sedan circling the reservation is simultaneously metaphor and real, in the way that Bigfoot, the tie snake, and other beings are metaphorical but exist. The black sedan was a warning symbol. It had the power to cross time when there was a crisis. A child considering taking their life is the utmost in crisis.

The appearance of the black sedan can also be expressed in mathematical equations or dynamic geometrical fluidity to make a sense of shape and time, but I am not fluent in those languages.

The mystery also makes sense in what you might call "chrysalis time," that place of deconstruction and reinvention, the place where wings emerge from chaos.

A year ago, I was at an event in Wyoming and spoke with a woman from Wind River. I told her this story that the young people had told me. She knew the story. It's true, she said. We all saw that black sedan.

4 First Memory

A friend told me that her first memory is being carried on the handlebars of a bicycle and seeing a mountain lion. Some have told me they don't remember anything until the first days of elementary school. When I hear that I assume that there must have been trauma, because trauma can cause memory dropouts. Or maybe these are the same people who say they don't remember dreams. I am convinced everyone dreams but not everyone remembers them.

In one of my first memories I was standing in my crib, my parents still asleep. It was not a day when they were up before I was, the weekdays when the clock cried and they jumped up and hurried about, my father getting dressed and my mother in the kitchen. It was one of the long mornings that followed the nights after they filled the house with friends, danced and partied, listening to all the top rock tunes on the radio. I'd be kissed, fussed over, tossed in the air to make me laugh, then put to bed. Through the evening my mother would crack the door and lean over to check on me as I slept.

One of those long-night mornings the curtains were

closed but a sliver of sunlight missed my sleeping parents and touched my face, made a triangle on the wall. I caught sunlight in my hands, and we played together, the sun and I. I danced back and forth along the crib bars, singing to my parent gods to get up and play. My mother started at the sunlight, heard my babbling, then leaned over the sleeping hill of my father to see me. She sniffed the air, and a frown crossed her face. She jumped up, grabbed me, and next thing I was naked under a forceful faucet of water in the bathtub. Maybe I remember this because in my good-morning baby mind I had been content, then a shadow of wrongdoing darkened it. It confused me. It was the first lesson in shame.

I have scraps of memory from even farther back. Maybe the memories don't coalesce in my conscious mind because they occurred before I had language. And I wonder how memories would shape differently if translated into Mvskoke rather than English. And maybe there are images and memories that defy any kind of language because they are not of this time and place, a time and place in which our senses function as knowledge bringers.

I have come to know that some of my memories aren't mine, rather come from other family members whose DNA spirals through my system. I have wrestled with a memory of being present at the Battle of Horseshoe Bend. In that memory I am not in the body that now carries my spirit. I am in the body of a distant grandparent who suffered seven gunshot wounds from Andrew Jackson's forces. In the terrible quiet I hear a redbird; I taste blood. I know that nothing will ever be the same. I could not imagine a future in the aftermath, but here I am now as the present speaking into the future.

Or maybe I catch moments of floating memories in the story field that rise up out of time because they want to be acknowledged, discharged, or find a place to plant themselves to grow.

When you hold a newborn and look into their eyes, you might see that they still carry memory of the story they are coming from. You might see the gifts they are bringing and have a sense of their story map. The early months in this life are about letting those memories dissipate so we can root into the present and embrace this story.

The approach through the doorway of early memory is unique in everyone. Some emerge into this story boldly. One granddaughter's eyes were wide open when she arrived. She keeps sentry even now when she is grown. Another child in the family preferred to sleep for most of her first months, then decided to take on her story full force.

When we have accumulated a lifetime of memories, we will head back in the direction of the doorway. All we will take with us are our memories. We will carry the story we have made during our time here.

I wonder about last memories. I imagine I will find that bit of sunlight and move with it until I am gone. I will go where there is no place for shame or regret.

5 Voice

When I first heard my daughter's voice in mine, I was speaking during a performance. I was surprised. I am not sure how to describe it. Her voice was distinctly hers, yet was blended into mine, different but the same. After that, her voice would often appear in my voice when I performed and then sometimes briefly in ordinary moments. I reminded myself that it was happening because she will carry on after I am gone, as will her children and their children. A mother and daughter after all make a continuum. I also noted how similar we were and sometimes so close that she fought to assert her own space in the overwhelm of my presence, of our legacy. Our push-pull was not unusual or particular to us, and common to mothers and daughters and fathers and sons.

You can feel the quality of someone's spirit in their voice. You can read a voice like a book or other kind of text. Voices carry residue of emotion even as they carry the pitch of expression. They vary from warmth to a far distant cold. Some voices are high and childlike. Others are deep with resonant power. Some hold back in their lack of trust of the world. Some push others away with a domineering quality. Our voices express our thoughts, dreams, and wants. Some might hide beneath trauma. Some tell the truth. Some lie. Our voices speak and sing our collective world into existence. Together our voices assist in determining the rise and fall of history.

One of my favorite relatives was my cousin Dona Jo Harjo from my father's side. She left Okemah, Oklahoma, and moved to northern California when she was a young woman, and like most Natives who leave their community, she often went back to the reservation. Whenever I visited her at her little house in Live Oak, California, we stayed up late every night talking and sharing, while her pet pigeon danced about in his cage on one leg. Mostly we discussed family and tribal history. She filled in my questions about her and my father's generation, and I would share what I had found in research and family visits.

We were pleased that our voices matched the same low resonance as our Aunt Lois's voice. Our aunt Lois Harjo was no longer living on this earth, but we kept her stories and memory alive as we spoke and carried on in these voices that marked us as close relatives. She was the center of many of our conversations. We were independent Mvskoke women, the members of our family who practiced art like our aunt Lois and her sister, my grandmother Naomi. We were motivated by the stories of our people and were proud that we continued long after government policies had been set into place to disappear and destroy us. We understood that our aunt, her parents, and theirs continued in us, and we celebrated that ongoing relationship every time we got together.

Even to speak someone's name was to bring them back again into our circle. This is why many indigenous cultures forbid speaking the name of those who have passed from this earth. Though we remember those who have gone, and they want to be remembered in a good way, it is important not to hold them too tight, or bind them with heavy emotion, as this can keep them from moving on to the next place in their journey.

When I heard my daughter's voice in mine, I knew she was with me, beside me, even though I might be physically far away. I could feel her as an intimate participant in what I spoke and performed.

After my daughter passed from this life, I wondered if I would ever hear her voice in mine again. I craved hearing her, but I would not be part of holding her back. I continue to surround her with protection and love as she continues her journey, as she assumes the role of an ancestor who brings rain.

Then, one night, months after she had passed this world, I briefly felt the presence of her voice in mine. And as I felt her voice, I also heard my aunt Lois, and my cousin Dona Jo.

It is the same voice that is the voice of my saxophone and

flutes, and just recently I began to hear my mother's voice in a similar manner, close to mine.

Writing these words is part of carrying on voice, a voice that is full of stories that gave us strength to survive, create, and keep going. I know that we are all together, that the stories of our people continue.

6 *Helpers*

One of my teachers who could see beyond time told me, when I went to him for insight, that he saw several helpers standing around me. Curious, he said, as he had never seen this before. They were lounging around, shrugging their shoulders, and showing him their empty hands. They had nothing to do because I did not call on them. I laughed to think of helpers mulling about and shrugging with nothing to do, because I certainly needed them. We all have helpers, he reminded me. They are there to be of assistance, but you must ask them. You wouldn't walk up to a counter in a coffee shop, he said, and just stand there.

This simple lesson has proven to be one of the most powerful. I have learned to ask for assistance in whatever I do. And I have learned there are many kinds of helpers, many specialists. It helps to be specific. Help always comes but it may not come immediately, and it may not be in the form you might have in mind. Make sure you have an open mind, an empty bowl, your pen or keyboard ready to receive or perceive it.

7 Ethics

The first time I remember tangling with an ethical decision I was about four. I remember the dress I was wearing. It was a sundress my mother had made me in fall colors. The skirt was gathered, and the front bib was a ruffled heart. The straps crossed in the back. I was proud of wearing my mother's love. It protected me. This love contributed to the choices I made throughout my life.

I was eating cookies. I had a cookie in my hand when a visiting friend of my mother's told me I had to share my cookie. I loved cookies almost more than anything, except my mother or my father. I didn't want to share and balked. In those times every adult had authority, even if they weren't your parent. They could reprimand and even spank you if they felt it was needed. In my memory I search for my mother in the room. I can't find her there. I would have looked to her. Nor do I remember the child with whom I was being urged to share.

This is when I became aware that I had a consciousness. I contemplated the woman's request to share but it was my consciousness, or spirit within, who gave me insight. I knew even without words—for that spirit within doesn't always use words—what I needed to do. My spirit showed me what would happen if I shared. It showed me how the child felt who didn't have a cookie and how sharing would make a trail of kindness between us. So, I shared.

I was also taught this by one of my mentors. Your spirit doesn't tell you what to do. It shows you the story. What you choose to do is up to you.

8 Romance

Like most girls of my generation, I wanted to forget myself and fall in love. We grew up with the dreams sold by the story-making machine of Hollywood movies and television. It was the same promise in the falling-in-love songs that sold and still sell and make hits. My mother penned this same kind of song as I sat at the kitchen table with her, of how romance was the beginning and the end. Romance promised the fulfillment of life for a woman.

Each love song or story in our collective atmosphere was a kind of spell that captured the minds of girls and young women. We believed that our dream lover would appear out of a mythical mist, either "tall, dark, and handsome" or a "blue-eyed devil" of charm. They would take you on dates, you would dance together in the moonlight, and one day he would propose, you'd marry, and then walk together into the perfect future of children and a house where love would root and live.

Many of the girls in my neighborhood had bride dolls to play out this dream. I ran from those dolls and play sessions and would go play with boys. We boxed, played war, or I'd test drive my brother's wheeled inventions. It's not that I didn't want to fall in love, but I didn't want that to be the be-all and end-all of my living. I wanted to be an artist. I wanted to travel. I wanted to play music in the circus band.

I study the black-and-white photograph of my parents' young romance. They are in a well-groomed Tulsa park. My mother's dark auburn hair falls over her sweater. My father is tall, dark, and movie-star good-looking. She fits precisely into his arms. This image embodied her romantic dream. They were young, they were in love, and they were the only two that mattered in their dreamy world. She had fled her home. He was out of military school without a mother.

Falling in love is a kind of ritual. There's the doorway of the dream and what it promises. You step through into a brightness of being unlike anything else: you feel taken over by a perfection you see in your beloved, by a possible future of happiness. You see only what is good in them, and everything around you is lit by that romantic haze. Anything is possible. There is no end. Forever is wreathed with roses that never wilt. I know. I abandoned myself in that ritual many times.

My parents were good dancers and frequented the big music and dance venues like the Casa Loma Dance Hall and Cain's Ballroom. In a photograph sleeve from one of the clubs is an image of my parents during their courting. They are a beautiful couple. His blue-black hair is styled with pomade enough to last the night. My mother has that falling-in-love glow. Yet there was also another sleeve, another image from the same night. There is a blonde woman in it. She looks flirtatiously at my father. He signals to her with his eyes that he will see her later, and the most painful part is that I can see my mother watching the betrayal bearing down. But she must have pretended not to see it, because they left the club together and walked into a precarious future.

I tore that image up in honor of my mother.

My mother fulfilled her dream of marriage with my father and had four children, two boys and two girls. That was her dream, she told me. And then it fell apart. Romance was not enough to hold it together. It never is—

Beware of placing your romantic dream on the back of someone who has no idea of your intention and isn't the least bit interested in your dream or you—or worse, who uses your dream to control you. Know your boundaries. Remember, you cannot change anyone. And if you only see the best qualities in someone, your dream will shatter when they prove to be human. If you are convinced your love will be enough to rescue someone, then you are almost fated to go down with them.

The romance myth that I grew up with was a dream unattainable by any mere human, nor did it include any partnership other than the convention of male and female. We are a diversity of identities on the identity scale. You are you and I am I, though some societies dictate that what's right for them is what's right for everyone. That's another disaster trail.

Still, I am a romantic. You can still fall in love and stay with a mate for life. It happens because there is also friendship, common goals, and compatibility. That need for intimate relationship with another is basic. That spark of connection we experience is real, and can be set off by looks, smell, intelligence, or any number of triggers of familiarity. It lightens the load of living. It makes us sing.

I decided to fall in love with creativity, with the beauty of the earth, with curiosity, with the questions that thread through human story making. I let go of the need to be elsewhere other than myself. Years later, love found its way.

9 Kitchen Table

When I was growing up, the kitchen was the warmest part of the house. The table is the heart. It's where we prepared food, cooked, hung out, and ate our meals. The kitchen table was a university of knowledge especially when it was filled with neighbors and relatives who shared food and stories.

Some of our best memories live at the kitchen table. Those are the ones made when favorite relatives and friends visit, and all the mothers and aunties gather around cooking, and you are called to help. You help pat out the fry bread or are charged with lifting the light brown circles from the grease. You cut up vegetables, stir the beans, and set the table. There's a roast or a bird in the oven. This is where the best stories are batted around. You find out about who is doing what, where, and with whom; you hear the good stuff about growing up. We knew the best stories would be pulled out when we children were shooed out of the room. We'd hide under the table to hear the forbidden. The tragedies are saved for later when the youngest children are asleep. When the food was done and everyone pulled up to the circle, they would give thanks, and everyone would gratefully dig in.

The table can also be a lonely place. The parents leave for work early, as both must work to afford rent and food. The children pour cereal and milk, then grab their bags and take themselves to school. Or there is only one parent trying to pull it all together. Even so there are barely enough funds for fresh food and childcare. Or the kitchen table is a seat in a car, a picnic table, or the bed in a cheap motel room for poor transits. Or there is no food, no table, just the street.

We can predict local and global economic trends by who is present at our kitchen tables, and what is set upon them. The kitchen table is an accurate gauge of cultural, social, and spiritual health.

For instance, when I lived on the island of Oʻahu I learned there are many kinds of bananas, not just the kind I grew up with that were stickered with multicorporate names. I began to question the story of how bananas found their way to my kitchen table. Who picked the bananas, and who grew and picked any of the plants that make it to our tables? Did anyone speak or sing to them? It matters, I've learned from the plants who live in my home.

And how did your food make it from the field to your table? Was it local or from lands far from where you live? And how were the animals raised and prepared? Were they respected and acknowledged for the gift of their lives? Were the workers respected for their labor? Were people paid a livable wage? Did they have humane living conditions? And what did we pay? And could we even afford to eat for health?

What was present at the kitchen table of my youth in many aspects is much different than what appears in the present. The fruits and vegetables today may lack the same nutrients because of soil degradation from pesticides and monocropping. I remember the early talks of acid rain. Our food animals are often raised in cruel circumstances and mass-produced in factory farms.

Or the table is littered with fast-food wrappers. Many don't even bother to cook anymore. Even the materials making the kitchen table have shifted from primarily wood to synthetic plastics. And what of the art of making anything, from the table to the eating utensils to the meal itself?

Consider too what words are spoken at the table. Do they become roots for war or are they the arms of our best dreams circling us? Why not invite respect and humility to come and sit at your table, kindness and understanding? And don't forget humor.

Finally, we are reminded to give thanks always for that which comes our way, first to the maker of all things for that which nourishes us, grows us—even that which challenges us, because how else do we grow our spirits? Remember to give thanks for the story keepers in your family and community. Don't forget to thank the cooks. Remember to put down your cell phone!

Perhaps the World Ends Here

The world begins at a kitchen table. No matter what, we must eat to live.

The gifts of earth are brought and prepared, set on the table. So it has been since creation, and it will go on.

We chase chickens or dogs away from it. Babies teethe at the corners. They scrape their knees under it.

It is here that children are given instructions on what it means to be human. We make men at it, we make women.

At this table we gossip, recall enemies and the ghosts of lovers.

Our dreams drink coffee with us as they put their arms around our children. They laugh with us at our poor falling-down selves and as we put ourselves back together once again at the table.

This table has been a house in the rain, an umbrella in the sun.

Wars have begun and ended at this table. It is a place to hide in the shadow of terror. A place to celebrate the terrible victory.

We have given birth on this table, and have prepared our parents for burial here.

At this table we sing with joy, with sorrow. We pray of suffering and remorse. We give thanks.

Perhaps the world will end at the kitchen table, while we are laughing and crying, eating of the last sweet bite.

10 Feeding Your Spirit

We are all fed by songs and stories throughout our lives, but it is in the coming-of-age years that we especially depend on music to mirror who we are, to carry us through all the angst and questioning that haunts us. Even though we hear music, feel it, can transcribe it by ear or script to perform, it is essentially spirit as it moves through, within, and around us and our environment. Every generation has its soundtrack of tunes that translate the essence of the times.

My favorite companion in my teen years was my transistor radio, which was about the size of my hand. I would hide under the covers at night with it and listen to local music stations as well as signals beamed in from larger cities like Oklahoma City and Kansas City. Most of the music I heard was from AM rock radio stations. FM was just beginning to figure in. My friends and I knew all the words and melodies and often sang together the songs, which were mostly about love and heartbreak. We played 45 and 78 vinyl disks on record players and our parents' stereo systems. We danced to what we heard in our homes or at Teen Town. These songs nourished our collective teenage spirit. The airwaves made an electronic circle of community.

When I accompanied my mother to the beauty shop located in a neighbor's made-over garage, the music came out of a radio perched on a shelf. Love songs were the backdrop while everyone suffered for beauty. As I listened to the banter, I found out everything that was going on in the community, especially when it concerned husbands and wives. In the afternoon, alcohol would find its way into the soft drinks or Kool-Aid, the radio would be turned up, and then the stories would grow wilder and more honest. There was so much laughter, which balanced the sometimes-tragic tales.

After radios came all manner of communication and listening devices, from cassettes to CD players, to cell phones, then digital signal and the ever faster and faster moving internet. Now we hear music from all over the world, from any era, instantly. Digital tracks are delivered in constant streams. We often listen alone, through headsets or earbuds, our singular worlds lit by a small screen.

Every generation in every community and culture has its trademark sound matrix. It is the basis even as we go forward in years. For my generation in the South–Southwest it was rockers, girl soul groups, Motown, British rock groups, singer-songwriters, psychedelic experimental bands. Then disco, world music, and, for some of us, blues and jazz classics became the foundation for hybrid reinventions. For Oklahoma Natives it was powwow and stomp dance.

Songs plant themselves more easily when our bones and minds are more pliable. We become part of the reach of music that is triggered by memory, just as songs trigger memory within us individually or generationally.

When I hear "White Rabbit" by the Jefferson Airplane I am on the lawn in front of the dorms at Indian school under the tall cottonwoods, kicking back with friends. I remember the Cherokee student Ron's prism glasses. He let me try them on. They replicated an acid high. How the world fractured beautifully. Imagination was always happening even if we couldn't see it with our straight minds. Our country was rupturing with discord over war and racial disparity and our Native Nations were making a stand for sovereignty by demonstration and fierce action. "White Rabbit" was not necessarily an anthem, but it embodied the spirit of the times.

As a student at the University of New Mexico, when the word was it was all going down at Wounded Knee in 1973, "Come and Get Your Love" by Redbone broke the airwaves. With that song it was as if we were all dancing around a drum with a circumference that connected all Native Nations. We saw ourselves as Turtle Island. My daughter was born the summer of that year, and I bounced her to this song to see her smile.

When I was a graduate student studying far from home in Iowa City, I remember a Saturday afternoon after cleaning house. My daughter was napping, and I could hear my son as he played with neighbor children outside the living room window. It was my time. I put on "Sketches of Spain" and lay on the floor near the speakers. The opening Spanish music chordal waves made a doorway, and I followed Miles Davis's horn through countries of tears, backwaters of blue, and found the root of the story in which I knew my people would make it through—

I was given nourishment of mind and spirit by the music.

When your body is hungry it searches for food.

When your mind is hungry it searches for art, literature, performance, and knowledge.

When my spirit gets hungry it goes to the mystery. It revels in sunrise and sunset. It drinks in mystery as it winds through the skies, the trees, and the grass. The animals all lift their heads as they listen. The insects begin singing. They all know the language of ancestors. It is music. Even Ekvnvcakv or Mother Earth sings. We are part of her song.

In turn, we must feed the ancestors. We give them offerings. We give them tobacco or corn pollen, we give them songs, we lift up prayers in remembrance. We listen.

11 Tricksters

We would have no stories at all if it weren't for failure, for bad decisions, or law breaking. Someone breaks into the house of the three bears and sleeps in their beds, a felon and predator becomes the leader of a country, or a demon is terrorizing a family in a house, still the family stays in the house. Only then do the stories unfold and show us, if they're well told, how to move through failure, bad decisions, or other trickery.

Human nature is naturally to be curious even if it courts danger. It is how we learn in this realm of duality. This is why we have trickster stories in every culture. These tricksters show us how we are when we misbehave, when we cross over into the liminal space between left and right, between dark and light. They remind us that power is something to be shared, not kept for oneself. Coyote never outsmarts Roadrunner, yet we are compelled by the story. There is a Coyote in each of us, even as there is also a Roadrunner. With our Mvskoke people, Rabbit or Cufe is trickster. There are many traditional Cufe tales, and then there are more contemporary stories, because that tension is ever present as long as we are in a world of polarity.

This is a contemporary trickster tale with roots that go deep into the past and even into the future. I wrote it before cell phones and earbuds were ubiquitous, now here we are—

Rabbit Is Up to Tricks

In a world long before this one, there was enough for everyone
until somebody got out of line.
We heard it was Rabbit, fooling around with clay and the wind.
Everybody was tired of his tricks, and no one would play with him;
he was lonely in this world.
So Rabbit thought to make a person.
And when he blew into the mouth of that crude figure to see what
would happen,
the clay man stood up.
Rabbit showed the clay man how to steal a chicken.
The clay man obeyed.
Then Rabbit showed him how to steal corn.
The clay man obeyed.
Then he showed him how to steal someone else's wife.
The clay man obeyed.
Rabbit felt important and powerful.
The clay man felt important and powerful.

And once that clay man started, he could not stop.
Once he took that chicken, he wanted all the chickens.
And once he took that corn, he wanted all the corn.
And once he took that wife, he wanted all the wives.
He was insatiable.
Then he had a taste of gold, and he wanted all the gold.
Then it was land and anything else he saw.
His wanting only made him want more.
Soon it was countries, and then it was trade.
The wanting infected the earth.
We lost track of the purpose and reason for life.
We began to forget our songs. We forgot our stories.
We could no longer see or hear our ancestors,
or talk with each other across the kitchen table.
Forests were being mowed down all over the world.
And Rabbit had no place to play.
Rabbit's trick had backfired.
Rabbit tried to call the clay man back,
but when the clay man wouldn't listen
Rabbit realized he'd made a clay man with no ears.

12 Stirring the Waters

Before I was seven, I had a difficult time calming myself when facing an upset. I would cry myself sick from disappointment or cruelty. Injustice was especially untenable, injustice like the death of a bird or of my little dog who chased cars and fell under the wheels of his prey, or like words said that did not feel deserved. I would usually cry alone as we were not allowed to make scenes, and I had my own pride. When I was older and upset, I could get lost in emotional chaos and despair. It could take hours or a day or so to ride it out. As a teenager, crackers in bed and music would calm me until I found my way. I came to realize that some situations would not be solved and the only way to change them was to leave home, something I was in no situation to manage yet. When I was much older, I would go to the water.

Our Mvskoke people are told to go to the water every morning and clean off. Water is essentially dissolved crystals. The water of the earth is our emotional field. Our bodies are mostly water. When you take a dip, covering your head with water, don't forget to thank the water for clearing you. This cleansing gives clarity. It refreshes your point of view, clears your mind.

Kaluahole Beach in O'ahu was my favorite place to go to water. I would take my one-man canoe out and jump off. The salt in the water and the wide movements of currents were especially effective in clearing me of discord, of any bad thoughts hanging on to me looking to feed off negativity.

If you are not near water and you are on an emotional edge, you can go to the sink, run the water, dip your hands in water and lightly cover your head with it seven times. You will feel calmer. Salt water is even better, and you can carry salt with you anywhere.

As I matured, I discovered that working out in the gym and dance classes, walking out in the natural world, and my artistic practice were also helpful in bringing me to calmer waters.

To know ourselves is the most profound and difficult endeavor. Though we are all made of the same questions, we have individual routes to the answers, or to reframing the questions. Why is there evil in the world? Why do people suffer, and some more than others? Why are we here? What are we doing here? What happens after death? Does anything mean anything at all? Who am I and what does it matter?

Sometimes we can get lost in the pall of the worst of human behavior.

Those days we might be tempted to retreat to the internet story feed to calm the waters of the anxiety. Yet in the unending scrolling story field on social media and the internet, we are witness to disheartening stories that instead feed anxiety and plant in us distrust and fear. There are also positive images and stories, but it is the negative that more easily lodges in our consciousness and stirs the waters.

I was reminded once by the Old Ones that when the waters are stirred up in a pond, stream, or river, you cannot see anything at all. When you are disturbed and cannot find rest within your mind, then stop stirring the waters. Thank the earth for her embrace, for holding you up. Feel your rootedness. Imagine the way the earth smells after a rain. Breathe in blue-sky clarity. Breathe out muddy confusion. Let your thoughts float. Do not follow them. The waters will grow still and clear.

When the waters are still and clear you can see into the situation with a more comprehensive point of view. You can see farther, deeper. As water's nature is to flow, it will all pass, all of it.

13 Friendship

One of my first memories is a girl staring at me as she stands in front of my house. This memory is so old it is made of mist. Her print dress gathers high on her waist, and she stands pigeon-toed and curious. I have never seen her before. We are three or four years old. Next is a garble of images: we are wrestling, we are running through the trees, we are laughing, and then we are physically fighting over the correct pronunciation of the word "the" and her mother is telling me to go home. The next day we are making a house out of her family's new refrigerator boxes. We were close until her family moved when we were in third grade. When she left, I was bereft. I no longer had a friend to walk to school with or to share days and hours with imagining and playing together.

Through my life I have been blessed with friends. In seventh grade I had quite the network of friends. Because the junior high was a feeder from several elementary schools, most of us didn't live near each other. We were quite a mixed economic and cultural group, from those who lived in smaller places in the more rundown neighborhoods farther away from school, like me, to those who lived in the larger fancy brick houses closer in.

Socially at our junior high we were divided between the "socs" and the "greasers." The socs were the popular upper-class students, held class offices and were often athletes or cheerleaders. The greasers tended to be lower class and often smoked along the back fence behind the school. My friends and I were neither socs nor greasers. I was known either as the artist or the brain. Another friend was a math genius, others were readers. Those of us who didn't fit in anywhere else fit in an odd togetherness. Some of us were Native. We didn't live near each other, but our school friendship helped us navigate those growing-into-ourselves times.

We were prodigious note passers. We had no cell phones then to text. One day in civics class my friends and I were passing a note bearing a lively discussion between us on the civics teacher and how often and why he scratched his manliness, which, of course, we couldn't help but notice. The note was in my hand when the teacher demanded I give it to him so he could read it aloud to the class. My friends and I froze. What was I going to do? I sat on the note. He asked again. I refused. There was no way I was going to let him read our note, especially to the whole class, even if I was sent to the principal or paddled. Our teachers paddled us back then, even in junior high. I wasn't afraid of it. I had been paddled before for chewing gum.

The teacher leaned back, scratched and moved things

around, then let the moment pass. Then he resumed talking about the structure of the Supreme Court. We were careful after that in his class when it came to passing notes. In our unspoken friendship pact, we would not give each other up.

I went to one year of high school with some of these friends before I left for Indian school in New Mexico. I've lost track of all of them. We were so close in those years. We kept each other's secrets and told each other things we could speak to no one else about, not even family. One of my friends lied about her age and danced in a club on weekends. She needed the money to leave her family for a better life. Another was seeing a man promising to take care of her. She was sixteen; he was in his thirties. I never heard from her again when she disappeared with him from tenth grade.

I am still friends with my high school friend Gloria Bird. We were in eleventh grade together at the Institute of American Indian Arts. She was the first person I ever met who called herself "a writer." We'd all be hanging out after class listening to music on someone's record player and she'd stand up and announce that she was going to her room to write. I admired her discipline.

A few years later we lived near each other in Santa Fe as struggling young mothers with small children. I would often see her with a baby strapped to her back as she bicycled around town. We eventually each moved from there but kept in touch for most of our lives by letters. We both went on to college with children as single mothers, and weathered relationships. It's all in our letters. I became a writer like her, and we both published books of poetry. We edited a Norton anthology of Native women's poetry together. We keep our friendship now mostly by email and phone calls. We have stood with each other through the heaviest moments of our lives. I can tell her anything. We don't see each other much because we live far apart on opposite ends of the country, but I depend on knowing she is there.

What characterizes my circle of friends at this time in my life is the willingness to dance at any moment when the right song appears no matter whether we are in a restaurant where dancing isn't allowed or on the steps of the Library of Congress; it is the willingness to wield fine-toothed honesty; show up anyplace with our rowdy and earthy humor; to share tears, clothes, or food; sing full-throated with mariachis if we know the songs; send flowers, cards, or surprises when it isn't someone's birthday; know each other's secrets and keep them; not hold our failures against each other; find a way through any disagreements, especially political or religious; be curious and ethical and fierce; back each other up in a fight and at the same time not drag each other into a foolish brawl; be generous with our hearts to our community, family, and friends.

Our friends are one important circle of belonging. They are as important as blood relatives, and often even closer, because we choose each other.

14 Fury

I've never known what to do with anger and fury. I am very respectful of it, even frightened by it, the way you would be if you were to find yourself in the presence of a fire-spitting dragon.

As a child I noticed that when I expressed anger, I got throat sick. That might explain my frequent strep throats, so frequent that a tonsillectomy was prescribed, and I refused it because, as I told my mother and the doctor, they were there for a reason.

Generally, I did not express emotions in a forthright manner. That was not our way in our family. I saw too much fury and anger acting out from my father and his friends. I saw what anger could do, how it sent me running in fear, or how it motivated me to act without thinking to protect my mother. I would sometimes cry my anger because I couldn't touch it with the right words. I would cry myself into illness, from fury. I would also hide out for safety and draw. I covered the garage with chalk art murals on slate walls as well as the walls of the closet I shared with my siblings. For the most part, I buried my own fury and hid from the fury of my father.

My stepfather's household had shifting rules. I was charged with keeping to his standards in all the chores assigned to me including laundry, ironing, washing dishes, and cleaning up. His standards were unknown until after a reprimand or a beating. And even then they changed from one day to the next. The injustice of it all made me furious. When I was pushed beyond my limits, I responded with words of outrage, questioning the truth of the matter, the lack of reasoning, the unfairness. My fury brought on more punishment.

That's when I turned it against myself. I cut myself. I drank some. I did what I could to numb myself. I was ashamed that I did not stand up to what infuriated me.

One morning it was time to get ready for school. My stepfather demanded that I find scissors that I had not misplaced or lost. You must find them now, he yelled. It was nearing time to leave to be on time for school. I was never late and almost never missed a class because school was my harbor, a safe place, and I found refuge in learning. I eventually located the scissors underneath one of my mother's piles.

When I returned to my room to dress for school, I pulled the drawers, one by one, out of my small pine chest, broke them and scattered my clothes all over the room as I searched for something to wear. No one but my sister saw me. She still remembers. I felt like a failure for letting go of control. I quickly picked up my clothing and pushed the drawer pieces back together and ran all the way to school. I came down with a strep throat the next day.

The last time I responded with an uncontrolled fury was when my son was small and I felt an unbearable pressure from trying to keep it all together with not enough money to cover rent, food, and expenses for school. The front door needed repair and kept sticking. I broke it down and tore it from its hinges. I remember the terror on his face, the fear, and I promised him and myself that it would never happen again, and it never did.

Not long after that incident I found a way to speak fury in poetry, a way to express the anger that was mine, and not just mine, but the anger that had climbed through generations of trauma that needed to be expressed, to be spoken for healing.

15 *Notice*

We see you, girl, with your baby in your arms. You were the star of your small-town high school. You carried the dreams of your mother, your grandmother, your community. You were set to succeed, accepted into one of the finest programs in the country for your discipline. You had a scholarship, scholarships. You were going somewhere far off the reservation to make a life that would shine against the cruelties of your living. You had already packed your bag. Bought some new clothes. You carried unknown secrets, burdens that no one knew or would have guessed because you buried them deep in the underground of your knowing. Some secrets were even unknown to you. You were going to leave them behind.

It was no secret you had a boyfriend. Others had entered your life briefly then disappeared. You knew he would eventually leave too. And then you were pregnant, you, the girl of your community's hopes and dreams. Of course you were going to have the baby and keep her. She was everything in your life now. You didn't know how. You didn't have a job; you'd have to get one. Your mother did the same thing, and you continued to live with her at home. The baby's father moved in with you, then you got married because it seemed the right thing to do. You were barely legal. He was there and then he wasn't there. He wasn't there even when he was there after he made a brief show of commitment. He grew angry. He'd had plans and now he had you and a baby he'd never wanted.

When she was born you saw life in a fresh way. With her, every increment of minute had meaning. You felt yourself in a kind of continuum that was unexplainable. Yet, everything around you appeared to fall apart. After a fight, the baby's father moved out. You moved in with your grandmother.

You signed up at the tribal college and were able to attend with a tribal scholarship. You began to hang out with people who were carrying their dreams forward, step-by-step. The baby learned to walk. She was quite the handful, like you, said your mother. Just like her and her father, your grandfather. As she grew up you took her to meet her father at a park or at a local restaurant. You didn't see him very often. You started learning your language again. It was your first language as a little girl, but with school and your life away from home you had lost much of it along the way.

You helped your grandmother prepare for ceremonies. She is a good cook. You stayed up all night with her, danced, helped serve, and cooked breakfast after the last dance. Still there were nights, loaded with homework, tired from work hours, and the baby sick with a stuffy cold and crying, that you thought you would not make it. It was too hard. And how would you ever make it? Your dreams seemed more impossible than ever. You didn't have the time you used to for your makeup and hair and didn't have the time or funds for the clothes that marked your style.

There you are in the thick of it, wondering if it is all worth it, if any of it really matters. You get up again, feed the baby, comb your hair, and walk out the door with your books and computer in your arm, your dreams by your side, urging you forward.

We see you. We hear you. We know you. We are you. We love you.

16 Songline

The bond with my daughter started even before she was born. I dreamed she came to me and asked me to be born. I saw her as she would be when fully grown, even as I simultaneously saw her as the baby who I would birth and raise up. I said yes even though the timing wasn't the best. I was a student with a young son, and her father, while happy about her birth, wasn't reliable. Her birth and babyhood were some of my happiest days yet some of the hardest because of the problems of making a living with little or no support.

I never liked leaving my daughter, at any age. Four days after she was born, I fastened her in her plastic baby carrier, placed her in the stroller, and walked to the university for my daily summer school classes where I was studying American Indian literature and linguistics. I dropped my son at childcare on the way. I remember him swinging his prized yellow school bus lunch box as he'd zigzag away from me, climbing over everything he could along the way, picking up rocks and sticks. Then I would go to my classes and work-study job.

I would nurse my daughter quietly in the back of the classroom with a receiving blanket draped over my shoulder. When fall semester came, I left her in the care of an elder Russian woman I trusted who wore her white hair tied back in a colorful scarf. Around her my daughter was calm and observant. My daughter would let me know if she didn't like someone or a situation, at any age, even from the earliest days.

My children were always on my mind as I made it through my day, but for my daughter I was always concerned about her security and safety. My son was always so self-assured, outgoing, and independent. My girl was inward leaning and always seemed to be keeping secrets, even as an infant. She was very sensitive. At two years old she sat on my lap in the movie theater and watched the hours-long *Dr. Zhivago* movie and cried in all the deeply emotional moments. That was my daughter.

When the fall semester started and I had to leave my baby at home, I would hurry back from classes, my son in one hand, a painting or books in the other. I could feel my daughter's anxiety as she waited for me, and because I was breastfeeding her, I would be full of milk. I'd pick her up immediately after I came in the door and hold her to my heart. I always had a panic about leaving her, even when she was grown with children of her own.

Any separation haunted us. I have notes in her childhood scrawl saying she missed me when I was gone for poetry residencies when she was young. I would sometimes cut trips short to return.

It was always like this with us, even during the years she closed in to make her own circle of family. She always wanted me close.

I write this as I fly out of the city in which she lived most of her life. I think about how complicated and contradictory we human beings are within ourselves and in our relationships with each other, especially the mother–daughter relationship. There can be such a push-pull because even as we are so much alike, we embrace our difference as a proof of strength and individuality, even as the so-called difference is in the end the same.

As the plane gains altitude, the lands below are the color of her skin. I see the house she lived in when her babies were small, near the tall building that housed the old Bureau of Indian Affairs office. And I feel her missing me as I miss her. She remains more present than ever in her earthly absence, in this phantom field of memory. This is the most painful separation of all. I have to fight the urge to go find her and bring her back into my arms.

I wrote "Songline of Dawn" when my daughter's life was full of young children, as I was once again leaving. The poem-song is for protection, for her and my grandchildren who were still sleeping as a flight I was on lifted and turned east over the Sandia Mountains. It remains a protection song, for them, for her. I am excited when I imagine hearing her steps, her voice, just as I am now when I hear the approach of my grandchildren and great-grandchildren. It is a way to be together, no matter where we are in the story.

We are ascending through the dawn
the sky, blushed with the fever
of attraction.
I don't want to leave my daughter,
or the babies.
I can see their house, a refuge in the dark near the university.
Protect them, oh gods of the scarlet light
who love us fiercely despite our acts of stupidity
our utter failings.
May this morning light be food for their bones,
for their spirits dressed
in manes of beautiful black hair
in skins the color of the earth as it meets the sky.
Higher we fly over the valley of monster bones
left scattered in the dirt to remind us that breathing
is rooted somewhere other than the lungs.
My spirit approaches with reverence
because it harbors the story, of how these beloveds appeared to fail
then climbed into the sky to stars of indigo.
And we keep going past the laughter and tears
of the babies who will grow up to become a light field
just beyond us.
And then the sun breaks over the yawning mountain.

And the plane shivers as we dip toward
an old volcanic field.
It is still smoldering
motivated by the love of one deity for another.
It's an old story and we're in it so deep we have become them.
The sun leans on one elbow after making love
savoring the wetlands just off the freeway.
We are closer to the gods than we ever thought possible.

17 Her Name

I have often wondered what use human beings are to the earth biosphere. We make trash mountains and pour waste into our waters as we participate in consumerism. We are burning the Amazon, the lungs of earth, and fracking for oil by dynamiting the earth, causing instability and earthquakes. We no longer take care of relationships with the spiritual guardians of the places in which we live. We have been taught that the earth is a dead thing to be mined for resources, with tacit permission by religious and secular laws to take what we want, whatever we need because we two-legged humans have dominion over the earth. We have taken and taken and continue to keep taking more than we need.

I remember hearing the warning years ago. When I was a very young woman, I attended Native elder circle gatherings to hear stories and prophecies. The elders foresaw climate change. They predicted the warming of the oceans, the melting of the polar ice caps. They predicted violent weather and floods that would result in loss of waterfront lands. They warned that the takers will keep taking until there is nothing left. They said that the circle would be broken if we forgot to take care of the earth and each other. They reminded us that we were part of the circle. Two-legged humans were not above all other creation. We were warned that we were at a crossroads and our actions would decide our future. This was more than fifty years ago.

We were reminded that a tipping point could be avoided if we recognized Earth as a living being, if we remembered she is our mother and treated her with the respect and love due her for all that she provides. Included was the proviso that each woman in our communities is a small earth. When earth and our women are respected, we will flourish. Where there is disrespect and mistreatment, we will all suffer in return.

Now here we are with evidence of massive climate change. Everything those elders warned about is coming to pass. Now I am part of the elders' circle and am passing on to you these same warnings. And one day, maybe your generation as elders will be celebrating how a new world came to pass, one of sharing, of everyone having what they need, a world in which every life form is respected, where the diversity of languages and cultures fuels society with connection, with *vnokeckv.*

My house is the red earth; it could be the center of the world. I've heard New York, Paris, or Tokyo called the center of the world, but I say it is magnificently humble. You could drive by and miss it. Radio waves can obscure it. Words cannot construct it, for there are some sounds left to sacred wordless form. For instance, that fool crow, picking through trash near the corral, understands the center of the world as greasy scraps of fat. Just ask him. He doesn't have to say that the earth has turned scarlet through fierce belief, after centuries of heartbreak and laughter. He perches on the blue bowl of the sky, and laughs.

If you look with the mind of the swirling earth near Shiprock you become the land, beautiful. And understand how three crows at the edge of the highway, laughing, become three crows at the edge of the world, laughing.

Don't bother the earth spirit who lives here. She is working on a story. It is the oldest story in the world, and it is delicate, changing. If she sees you watching she will invite you in for coffee, give you warm bread, and you will be obligated to stay and listen. But this is no ordinary story. You will have to endure earthquakes, lightning, the deaths of all those you love, the most blinding beauty. It's a story so compelling you may never want to leave; this is how she traps you. See that stone finger over there? That is the only one who ever escaped.

18 The Race

We gathered on the beach at our outrigger canoe club, waiting for the call of the officials as to whether we would race or not. There was a small-craft warning. The winds were demanding as they swept over the coast. They had muscle. I had gotten to know some of the winds there. There were many winds, each with Hawaiian names. I never learned their proper names but came to know some of the different personalities of the winds. The winds involved in the small-craft warning were island-hopping winds. They were young male winds with a strong push.

Because I travel so much through the skies, through cloud territories, I've come to know that winds have places they live, and characteristics that mark them, often related to certain directions. They can be very responsive to humans as their nature is to be responsive. One time a hurricane was heading toward the island of O'ahu where I was living. We got news that it had veered away out into the ocean. That morning after the news a Tahitian healer visited. She commanded us, "Feel my hands." You could feel wind energy on them. She told us that she and others on the island had prayed the hurricane away.

I've learned, in all my flight travel, that the winds like to be greeted. They appreciate being acknowledged. When the pilot announces turbulence and asks the flight attendants to be seated, if you ask the winds' involvement, they will often cooperate and let you down easy. Most winds are helpful, many are playful, and some are punchy young ones, like the winds who were muscling their way around the island the day of our race.

We were finally given the go ahead to start, and at the crew meeting as we huddled in a circle near the canoes, we were again reminded of each of our six positions in the canoe. I was in seat five, the keeper of the *'ama* or outrigger to the back of the canoe. If the waves or the winds push the *'ama* up, the canoe will flip. And in an unruly ocean it can be difficult to right the canoe and get out of the wave zone. The ocean, we were reminded, would be gnarly and everyone would need to be especially alert.

Seat one, in the front, is the eyes of the canoe. This is also the stroker seat, for the one who keeps the time of the canoe. All paddlers must enter the water, and move together with each paddle stroke in sync, or the canoe won't move smoothly, or will hardly move at all. Seat two is in tandem with seat one. They each paddle on different sides, adjusting the stroke based on the winds and waters. Seat two also calls the changes, for switching paddling sides. Seats three and four are called the power seats. Usually, the larger and more muscular paddlers are placed here. Seat four is the person who bails if the canoe goes over. Seat five also assists. Seat six is the steersperson, the captain of the canoe. They steer the course, again taking into consideration tides, waters, and winds as well as what's going on with the crew and the canoe.

Even before we put our outrigger to water, our adrenaline was firing. By the time we were lined up for the race with all the other clubs and the start was given, we were ready.

As we had anticipated, it was a grueling race. I learned that water is always different every time you go out to paddle, though each area had recognizable characteristics based on land formations, depth, and how forces were configured in each area. There were also wind relationships and moon phases to consider. That day the waves were high with tremendous push. Even at our start I had to make a solid lean on the *ʻama* so the canoe wouldn't *huli*, or flip. Our steersperson kept a well-placed line through the current as we made that sweep around the island. We saw two canoes flip as we maneuvered through the rough action. To get a canoe going again in those kinds of waters requires cooperation and strength in the battle of winds and waves.

During my few years of racing outrigger canoes I came to understand that so much of a race is in your mind. You need training, muscle, and good ears yet almost just as important, in a race or anything else you do, is an attitude in which you know you will see it through in the best manner possible. You will give it everything you have to give. You imagine the best possible outcome and, when and where possible, you make friends with the forces you need to work on your behalf, like the winds.

When we made it to the finish line at Ānuenue, my first canoe club, where I learned to paddle under the direction of the master waterman Nappy Napoleon, we were exhilarated. As we pulled up to the beach, the end of the race, we were lit up with the accomplishment of all that it had taken us to keep the canoe moving and upright through heavy winds and waves. I had played only one small part, but every one of us had been necessary to making it to the finish line—even the canoe. Each canoe has a spirit and is fed and honored for its purpose.

Because of that race I came to understand why people pushed themselves beyond their limits in sports or any other test of physical skill and endurance. I was surprised that I fell even more in love with the waters of the Pacific. I gained trust in my crewmates, and I also gained trust in myself and how I moved about in and with the ocean. She was one of my most important teachers.

Oh, and by the way, the way I remembered it, we placed in that race.

19 Thought Trails

I had just finished a one-hour spin class and was full of sweaty energy. I was feeling accomplished for making it through with a tough instructor, when I noticed the thought, "I want a doughnut." I had cut doughnuts out of my diet years earlier. It was unusual for such a thought to enter my thought stream. When you consider how many thoughts drift through your mind daily, even hourly, or by the minute, you could be overwhelmed by thinking so many thoughts. When the image of the doughnut demanded attention, I decided to investigate the thought. As I held it in my mind, I noticed it had a trail. I followed the trail, and it led me to the man on the bike next to me, who was vigorously toweling off. I realized it was his thought, not mine. That a thought might not be mine was quite a revelation.

I began to question where my thoughts were coming from, and even where they were going. What I learned is that thoughts are everywhere there are humans. Most thoughts just pass us by, like the one in the spin class; they don't make it to our consciousness because they aren't sent directly to us. Similar thoughts in your mind field might like the company and if there are enough of them, together they can make things happen.

If a thought is directed to you, it has an address and will find you. A thought of good intention will lift your spirit. A thought meant to harm can work like a dart or a punch. We each have a natural armor of protection that is strengthened by prayers, positive thoughts, fresh food, and good company. But negative patterns like addiction wear holes through this protection and can eventually destroy it. That's why you often hear that someone is so different when they're high, drunk, or otherwise taken over by a drug or stimulant. They are different. It may not be them speaking or acting. Keep in mind that after your own thoughts go out, they eventually return to you. When they return, they are often more weighted because they've gone out and made friends.

Thoughts are part of the overall energetic field and like all stories, they work toward harmony. Consider the power of thinking in a group. Wars begin this way. One negative thought can feed another, and when they congregate, they can cause harm. Consider the power of widespread initiatives of peace from leaders like Gandhi, Martin Luther King Jr., and the Honorable Dalai Lama. Those thought waves embolden efforts for peace and connection.

As I began to pay attention to thoughts, I learned that not all thoughts originate with other humans, but instead many come from animals, plants, and other living beings. They are harder to hear because their frequency is very different from thoughts made with human languages. The first time I heard plant thoughts was the day my mother asked me to unload a plant she had picked out and set it on her porch. When I set the plant down, I heard plant voices telling me, "We don't want that plant here!" At first, I didn't even question that I heard their voices because I was so shocked that these plants, all making beauty with flowers, were being so negative. I spoke back to them with my mind and told them that they shouldn't act this way. They should be welcoming to this new plant. But I listened to them and moved the plant to another place on the porch. There was quiet and I left that plant there, where it flourished.

In retrospect, there may have been reasons behind the protest of the plants who were living on my mother's porch. Maybe the incoming plant was not compatible to their species, and it could have been carrying something harmful to them.

There is antipathy and attraction in all living things, even plants or planets.

What of thoughts that are unlike any other thoughts that have been here before, thoughts that are innovative, that bring into the world renewal, invention, and fresh understanding? They might first be seen as threatening, too revolutionary. The world was flat, then it was round. Women are not smart enough to vote. Indigenous peoples are not human, they are fauna. There are many stories about what happened to people who dared speak innovative thoughts when change was not welcomed. And yet often these kinds of thoughts are exactly what a culture or a people require for growth.

We need fresh thoughts that revive our tribal nations and all cultures, that encourage connection, that bring into recall words of our languages, thoughts, and ideas that we thought were lost but instead were just needing new vehicles to carry them. These are thoughts born of our family dreaming, the dreaming of nations, and of ancestors. Here you will find the story field where poets, artists, thinkers, dreamers, and children create. Our ancestors' thoughts are still here, but you will leave your own tracks.

20 Rainbow Speak

I was living in ʻĀlewa Heights on the island of Oʻahu. The house was on a road that led to a ridge from which you could see almost the whole island and beyond. From the window of my workroom, you could see the sweep from downtown Honolulu to my south out past the airport to the west. I must have been writing, because when you are in creative space the doors of perception swing wide so that you have access to larger, timeless realms. I paused in the momentum because I heard a voice—not a human voice and not in the airwaves outside my ears, rather from the intuitive realm.

"Come out and see me," urged this voice that was not a human voice, and not a scary or a frightening voice, but the voice of a kind, light frequency. I was curious as to who was speaking so I followed the voice. I left my workroom and walked down the hall to the lanai and, arched in the sky over and beyond the neighbor's house, over the banana trees, was the rainbow. She had called me out to see her. She was as beautiful as ever as she arched in the sky from the Koʻolau Mountains to the ocean. I wondered why this was the first time I could hear her. I took a photograph of her to remember that day.

That the rainbow spoke and could speak marked a profound change in my awareness of communication being possible between humans and elemental forces like clouds, rain, and winds. In the prevailing Western belief system, two-legged humans are the only ones endowed with the ability to communicate. Yet, because of the rainbow and other experiences, I have learned that communication is ongoing among all living things—animals, plants, the elements, and even the stars. We also know this is possible from the stories that have accompanied and formed most indigenous world cultures. Now even the sciences can prove that there is communication among all living beings.

After that initial encounter, rainbows continued to teach me. They showed me that though they might disappear, when they reappear in the same area, they are the same spirit. They go where they are needed and when the conditions call them into being. This was given to me by a rainbow on Kaua'i in Waimea Canyon at Kōke'e State Park. She disappeared and reappeared twice to show me.

Another time a rainbow spoke to me was in Albuquerque, New Mexico. I was in the backseat of the guitar player Larry Mitchell's van, heading south to Los Lunas for a visit and photography session with our friend the photographer Karen Kuehn. As I watched out the window a rainbow appeared to the east, in front of the Sandia Mountains. I heard the rainbow say, "I will see you later and I am bringing someone with me." I was still surprised the rainbow had spoken to me. I kept it to myself, of course.

It was very late afternoon, a perfect light, and the three of us went out onto the bosque for the image making. Then as Karen shot her characteristically beautiful images, behind us a double rainbow appeared, in a stunning double arc. There was the rainbow, as she had promised, with the other rainbow she'd promised to bring.

I have heard rainbows speak since, but not very frequently. One day recently here on the reservation I was missing rainbows. I hadn't seen one in too long. The islands have a heavy rainbow population but here in the middle of the mainland, not so much. As I drove west, and seemingly in response to my reverie on the scarcity of rainbows in my recent life, a rainbow appeared. "We are still here," it said, and then disappeared.

I don't know why the rainbows spoke to me. Maybe because I would remind you and be reminded that we are in a living story of manifestation and communication. I am at the age now where many of my teachers were when they passed on their knowledge to me. I am now passing this on to you. Even stories ripen. There might be something here that will help you as you navigate a very changed world in which people have forgotten that we are part of a living planet, a living system. Each of us has a voice and a presence. No one is above the other.

21 *Be Yourself*

I am frequently asked what advice I might want to pass on to young poets, writers, and musicians. What often appears in my mind at this question is an image of sunlight flowering the living room from a skylight in an adobe condo near the Rio Grande. It was one of my favorite places to live. A giant aloe vera plant thrived under the skylight. She was surrounded by her children.

One of my mentors had come by for a visit. She was an older Pueblo woman, close to my mother's age. She was deeply spiritual, guided by her Pueblo beliefs and by Pueblo Catholicism. After some catching up about family, she motioned to the aloe vera plant. She spoke about the wisdom the plant was carrying. She advised that if I were to put myself in the place and mind in which the plant existed and knew, I would know myself.

Only now, when I am nearly my mentor's age, am I beginning to understand what she was sharing. The plant had never lost her connection to the earth. She was humble as she drank sun and the water I would give her. She was grateful to be an aloe vera plant and did not try to be anything or anyone else. She did not have to strive to be who she was; she just was who she appeared to be.

Then before my friend got up to leave to do all the errands she had to do in town before returning to the pueblo, I expressed some kind of anxiety over a performance I had coming up. I used to have near debilitating performance anxiety. She looked at me intensely and said, "Just be yourself."

Those words, that phrase, sound so simple, so elementary, yet that was exactly what the aloe vera plant was doing, what most of creation was doing, except for us often insecure two-legged human beings. We too often question our existence and find it too easy to point out the flaws in others as we stumble along. Yet when we are exactly ourselves, we flourish. You must find and nurture your spirit. You must make your own path. You must be yourself.

22 *Performing*

Like many of you, I was terrified of speaking in public. In elementary school my speech class required that we stand in front of the class and perform. I suffered through that class. I was miserable. Because I didn't want to fail, I forced myself to participate. Yet it wasn't the same with acting in school plays. I was often chosen for parts because the teachers agreed that I had a voice that carried. I enjoyed performing as someone else, a character.

When I began writing poetry as a college undergraduate, I didn't have any trouble reading my poem drafts to the class because we sat close around the seminar tables in the classroom. The circle felt intimate because our poetry professors made the art accessible even as they stressed craft. We read the poems of many fine poets in class and attended poetry readings together. I flourished. I engaged deeply with the sound art of poetry. Soon I was asked to visit other classes to share my poetry. There weren't many Native women writing poetry like mine in which I confronted contemporary Native issues in a unique voice. I was fearful as I read in front of classes, but keeping the pages of poems in front of my face gave me something tangible to hold.

As I finished my undergrad years and went on to graduate school, I began to receive many requests to read and perform my poetry. The larger the venues and audiences became, the more fear of performing I had to negotiate.

A few years after I received my MFA degree from the Writers' Workshop at the University of Iowa, I was invited to speak at the Heard Museum in Phoenix, Arizona. It was an honor to be invited to read at a place so prestigious and important to Native arts. I was also excited that Wynema Torrans Posey, the daughter of the famous Mvskoke poet Alexander Posey, was in the room. Knowing that made me even more nervous as I paced back and forth in the makeshift green room, while the audience was being welcomed and seated. My stage fright had matured and grown quite large since elementary school. I nervously checked out the exits as I briefly considered fleeing. I told myself to get myself in control. I took a deep breath and asked for help. A thought came that said if I made the stage my heart, and imagined everyone as part of my heart, there would be no place for fear. When I performed that day, fear was not in that room. I even enjoyed the performance.

I was almost forty when I took up saxophone and essentially learned to play by playing onstage. My fear was compounded because you cannot hide while playing saxophone. It is a loud, even obnoxious, horn, with an unmistakable voice. Stage fright now took me on higher levels of challenge. This added a tremendous amount of stress to my poetry performances. Yet, I loved what the saxophone added, as music can transport the words into that place beyond words, the place where the best poems live.

I was featured at the Tucson Poetry Festival with two band members I enjoyed playing with, Keith Stoutenburg, a songwriter and guitarist, and Michael Davis, the bass player of MC5 out of Detroit. We were doing well with our set, but stage fright sent me into overthink. I fixated so much on the fear of playing something wrong that this took me out of the music. I abruptly stopped playing in the middle of a song. It took all the strength I had to keep from running off the stage in humiliation.

After the performance, when I had calmed myself down, my common sense told me, you don't have to play, and if you want to play then find a way. I wanted to play. I had quit music in my teens when a band teacher wouldn't allow girls to play saxophone. And now in the middle of my life, I'd picked it back up. Because saxophone was relatively new to me, I decided I would play at every performance, even if it wasn't a music performance, just to get over my fear. And the more practice I had with my saxophone, the more my confidence grew. Still, I grappled with performance anxiety.

A few years later I was asked to take part in a large performance in San Francisco with professional musicians and singers. I was invited because of my poetry, not because of horn playing. Still, I was given an eight-bar solo. Whenever I ran my solo in my practices at home, I kept imagining all the mistakes I was going to make. Of course, I made all those mistakes at the rehearsal. I had practiced them very well. There is no mistaking the deadening sound of failure when you are with players who play.

I went back to my room and checked all the departing flights for home. I couldn't get out until after the performance. As I sat with my common sense, I understood that I had to rethink the solo as successful. I went over and over the solo and the next night my small musical moment went without notice. The featured singer, Faye Carol, gave me an unexpected lesson that has held me to this day. She sang soulfully with joy. She became the audience and the audience became her. She wasn't worried about mistakes or what she looked like: she just listened to the music.

Since then, I have learned that the audience, the place, the staff, the organizers are all essential components of a performance. When you come into a space, ask permission of the space and all the elements of the space. Say who you are and what you are there for—in other words, speak your intention. Acknowledge the land and those who keep the land as you walk around the space before the performance. Ask that the space be blessed, that those who need to be there find their way. Speak good words for the room, the staff, the sound people, the organizers, the other musicians, and those who are coming as audience. Give gratitude for the opportunity to share, and ask for inspiration. Make sure you are practiced, have all your equipment in good shape, and are ready.

I often dance in the green room before going on, to move the energy through and around my body. I feel out the audience, something I do often before I get there—but it's always important to read the energy at hand. I remind myself that I am there for a reason, to be a participant, and I lean in with curiosity. I have a set list, but I will change it or even ignore it once I get onstage when something else is needed. I ask for spiritual assistance. Then I do what a drama teacher taught me: I draw an imaginary line between life and performance, and then cross the line into the magic liminality of the stage. I listen to the music and play.

23 Failure

When I am introduced to an audience, and the host reads an extended overblown version of my resume and accolades, I often remind the audience that my list of failures is much longer—that, in fact, it might scroll down the podium, through the audience, and out the door.

When improvising in music, a wrong note can become a step to a phrase that will transform the tune, all in time. Miles Davis said, "There are no wrong notes . . ."

Every story has infinite possible versions. Every step leads you in a direction. To get to where you need to go, you need clear intention and need to arm yourself with knowledge, attitude, and resilience, because it is guaranteed you will face pushback, you will fall, and you might find yourself at the bottom of a pit with no apparent way to get out. You might be told it is impossible, that your skin color is wrong, or you aren't what's popular and in vogue. Maybe you are too old or too young. This is when you hone your skills of listening. You listen to common sense. Make lists of what you hear. You listen to your spirit. You learn to make ladders, to go to the depths of understanding within yourself.

I'd rather fail magnificently while trying than not even try at all. Every work of art, every fresh idea that nourishes the community is littered with what are called failures.

There would be no story without mistakes. Give chase. Be curious.

24 Contradiction

We each embody origin stories. Some of us emerged from the earth after a world was destroyed by our wrongdoing. We may have come from the stars and now carry star knowledge. Some of us may have been formed by a lonely male god who took the rib of a man and made a woman to accompany him. Others honor mothers and their essential stature as they forge life. All of us emerged through the door of the earth, or a mother. These origin stories are rich with mythical metaphor and form the basis for many systems of knowledge.

All origin stories begin with attraction and opposition—a clash. For something to manifest in the world you need electricity, force, and magnetism.

We each have our personal origin stories. They form a basis for our own personal belief system, for better or worse. For any story to exist in this realm, it must embody contradiction to root.

My personal family origin story embodies class and race clash. My mother's family were sharecroppers, from mostly European settlers and unenrolled Cherokee. We still have an iron pot that was brought over on the Trail of Tears. One side of my father's Mvskoke family was rich from Indian oil money. Some of their allotted land lay atop a major oil field. My great-grandfather had the first automobile in Okmulgee, Oklahoma, and he even established Harjo Oil Company. When my parents came together there was bound to be clash.

When I was a child, at least once and sometimes twice a year we visited my mother's parents, who lived in a one- or two-room sharecropper house. That part of my origin story is characterized by the smell of kerosene from the lamp on the kitchen table and the flickering light on the walls of the small house. When we went to the outhouse at night it was so dark we could not see anything in front of our faces. Our ears would immediately open wider to pick up what sight couldn't uncover.

The small farm included chickens, ducks that would swim in a half-tire circle filled with water, sometimes a cow, and a pigsty of always hungry pigs that we were warned would eat us if we fell into their pen. Of course I was drawn to the pigsty by that story, and I would lean over their wood enclosure and pet their perceptive snouts, all of them snorting and pushing at my hands to see if I was bearing anything to eat. I loved riding in the back of my grandfather's barely running pickup balancing the tall, empty water cans as we drove to fill them directly from the spring that poured sparkling through the rocks. There was a lake nearby where we fished. I always tangled my line and needed help from my patient grandfather. I preferred wading out and catching crawdads or swimming. The Bible was the only book in their house and in it, scribbled in pencil, was written the genealogy of the family. My grandparents were poor, but they gave me some of the richest memories of my young life.

The other side of my origin story is my father's family. My father was raised in a twenty-one-room house in Okmulgee, on the Muscogee Creek Nation Reservation. His mother was a full-blood, and her family were educated. They were from those who fought for justice, were tribal speakers and leaders. My father's mother passed from this world when he was young, and he was sent to military school by his father and stepmother. My father's family wasn't happy that he was marrying the daughter of sharecroppers.

One of my grandmother's sisters, Lois Harjo, was my mentor and teacher. She taught me Mvskoke culture and was my favorite relative because she had stories and valued art, creativity, and history. Her apartment in Okmulgee was my favorite place and still is in my memory. It was full of art, stacks of books, and family papers containing tribal history and stories.

We were quite the pair as we drove around the Creek Nation visiting relatives and listening to stories. I remember going to Wewoka, the capital of the Seminole Nation in Oklahoma, to visit a Chupco relative who knew how to make medicine. He could see what couldn't be seen by others. Often, we'd visit George Coser Sr., a cousin, who was the best storyteller and told stories in the manner of Will Rogers Jr., complete with a lariat. He had even performed for royalty in Europe. Within these family stories I found community and connection.

When we're young and in the throes of making our own way and creating our own stories, we often discount our family origin stories as not having much to do with our lives because we are in a very, very different world than our parents and grandparents. We are not them and don't want them interfering. We might think we know more than anyone because we are the authorities in the realities we've constructed with music and our own generational thought field. Yet every generation is in relationship to the other. A child's generation hopscotches over to the grandparents' generation. Our parents' generation leaps over to connect with the great-grandparents' generation. They find commonality and even relief in their shared story. Parents and children are often too close to get the best overview of the quantum tale. We build our generational stories often out of clash from the previous generation, and maybe we need this energy and what it generates to build.

I've come to believe that every generation is a kind of person. You come into the world together, a connected wave of humanity, to experience knowledge and history as a singular entity. My generation was marked by the Cuban Missile Crisis: we were taught to duck-and-cover in school, were wary of nuclear destruction. We were further shaped by the British music invasion, Motown, and the protests raging against war, racism, and poverty. We fought for Native rights. We defined ourselves by styles of music, as does every generation.

Every moment in time is a point of origin. Something is always happening. There is always change. When the story feels overwhelming, burdensome, too much to carry, remember every moment is some kind of origin point, a new beginning. Pay attention. Take out the earbuds or earphones. Shut down the computer. Make an altar to an ancestor whose story inspires your own. Give gratitude for those who made it through the trails of tears, through clash. Keep walking.

25 Intimate Violence

Acts of intimate violence are among the most difficult to reckon.

You are thrown to the floor by a drunken father, an uncle, or a date, and you are violated, broken. And worse, you aren't believed or you are blamed. Or you are threatened with your life if you tell, or your family's life is threatened, too. Or you have gone out with friends for drinks and dancing, or to a fraternity or student club party, and when you resurface to consciousness you find you have been roofied and raped. Or you drank too much, and it happened, and you blame yourself, not those who took advantage. You could be any age, from infancy through adulthood. What do you do with something so unthinkable, unspeakable, unbearable?

We women are the center of power for our communities, and we carry the center of power in our bodies and for our families. When there is such a violent violation enacted against us, not only do we suffer, but so does the very spirit of our communities. When a community condones disrespect of femaleness, then there will be no peace. Everything will fall apart from within. The hatred of what is female is a betrayal of the gift of life force. Nothing good follows and the society that disrespects the giver of life will implode in time because the pillars that are needed to keep a house together will not be standing together.

You will need all the warrior courage you can muster to move forward after intimate violence. You will need words for girding. You will need tools for defense like time and belief in your power to heal. You will need the arts, words, and physical discipline to strengthen your body.

You will know it is time to face the brokenness when you realize you are acting out with sexual aggression or promiscuity, compulsive behaviors, and self-harm. When you see that you are putting yourself in dangerous or compromising positions because you have forgotten or misplaced your value. When you are tired of being so depressed or low-spirited that all you want to do is eat fast food and snacks, play video games, or watch videos on social media. When you are defensive when there is no need to be defensive, or when you have lost your voice, or even your dreams. And if all this happens before you have acquired language, then the haunting will be more difficult to uncover, to heal, because the words are almost impossible to call forth to undo the spell of harm.

I remember when I made the turn in the direction of healing. It was probably a Sunday morning. It might have been after a party where there was blood and broken glass in the parking lot from a fight that broke out.

I don't know what made it different that morning, except that my soul was tired. I felt ugly. I felt like I never fit anywhere. I know I wasn't the only one. A foreign way of thinking and being had forced its way into our minds, emotions, and our bodies, and even into our own tribal cultural structures. Education and the city had changed us and often made us unrecognizable at home. We'd come together to sing songs in the languages we were told were wrong or illegal, that we were forced to leave behind for a certain shape of civilization. We came together to remember the best parts of ourselves. But we could not forget the worst no matter how much we tried.

I had to learn to reach out for help. It was difficult because in my family no one spoke about these things that harmed us. We just tucked them in the place we hid all shame and kept going, but like any secret the memories emerge, often at inopportune times. I found assistance from counselors and healers. I studied poetry, esoteric texts, and stories, and listened to music. I painted and wrote. I made friends with my dreams. I began to gather the pieces of myself that I had lost or that had broken off and needed to find their way home to wholeness. There were starts and stops, successes and failures along the way.

It was when I decided to embrace all the parts of my story

rather than fight them, that the healing took hold. I had to learn to accept the story of all that I had been through, even the worst parts. I came to understand that these parts, though they were destructive in nature, had something to offer. They were teaching me empowerment.

I am still working on the story. What I have learned and am learning I am passing on to you. Sharing what you learn is an important part of the process toward healing. What we heal within will also heal the upcoming generations and will even reach back to heal those who have come before us.

26 *Making It Through*

When you can no longer fit words to turmoil. When the sky is gray even when there's sun. When time is a sieve fed by nothingness. When there's no forward or backward. When your heart stops making any music you can hear—

You might think no one sees or hears, that no one understands. You've turned your back.

I want to use these words to go beyond words to the place where your spirit has made a home in your gut, so I can help bring you back into the circle, to those who love and honor you no matter what has ever happened, no matter what you think you have done to deserve any harm. I want the intention behind these words to reach beyond the physical borders of a book or a screen, to make it through mental and emotional fences, through the walls that were built with materials made by words and actions of ill-meaning relatives, teachers, or other bullies from childhood, from any lifetime, from anywhere in history, or from anyone who has walked through genealogy to find you to pass on harm. Even one small word can make an opening in the dark, and you can begin to smell the pines of your homelands, fresh flowers, or the aroma of grateful earth after a much-needed rain.

I have been where you are now in the overwhelm, lost in the heavy forces of despair, without family, without resources, without any sure path through chaos.

Once in time I was in a back-and-forth struggle with my baby's father. When not drinking he was brilliant and helpful, a good cook. When he would drink, it felt dangerous to be around him. Negative thought forms began eating my fear, growing larger and larger. That's how I found myself curling into a reality marked by terror and panic, and I became afraid that I might cause harm more to myself than to him.

One late afternoon I had to fight with myself to keep from driving off a bridge. When walking home from school I huddled on the median to keep myself from running into traffic. I was sitting in a literature class when I realized that I was going to break into a million little pieces. I didn't know what it would look like or how it would happen, and I didn't want whatever was going to happen to be in front of my class, so I slipped out of the room and walked straight across campus to the student counseling center. I asked for help.

From childhood I had learned that I had to depend on myself, that no one would be there if I did call out. My parents loved me, but they were caught up in their dramatic and violent stories. Then my mother married a predator. I knew then I was on my own whatever happened. Some nights were overwhelming in those years. Prowlers harassed our house and my bedroom. My body was changing. I began to cut myself. I don't know where I got the idea. It was the beginning of a trail to suicide; it was a cry for help. When I cut, I felt release. I stopped when my mother came in one night and yanked back my blankets and saw what I had been doing. The look of dismay, shock, and sadness on her face said everything. I stopped, even though no words had been passed between us.

When I discovered the power of words to heal, to invent new worlds, to open pathways of fresh understanding, I began writing poetry. "Word" and "world" are permutations of manifestation and reach. With skill, words could intercede between chaos and calm, through immovable density to sunrise. I found a voice, where before there had been none. I found release to step outside the bondage of destructive thinking.

As I wrote, I could hear beyond everyday frequencies. Writing was an act of call-and-response. I listened to the worlds around me, to the worlds inside, and then wrote in response. I learned I was a witness of time, place, and cultural shift. Poetry taught me how to write what could not be spoken, what needed to be spoken. What was wise that came through was given because it was what I needed to hear.

I am convinced that artists are directly involved with

the ancestor and other spiritual realms. Everyone has roots there, but artists hone communication and bring back art to share.

I speak with an urgency now because I want you to know you can find a way to the other side of despair. You have ears that perceive frequency beyond the physical barriers of time. You can hear your ancestors, those who love you, those who helped set you on your journey here and are always here for you. You might hear them in poetry, in music, in the words of our friends, your family. They are reminding you that you will be tested, that you are being tested because you are strong and beloved and because your spirit is growing muscle so you can help others. They remind you that you were made of *vnokeckv* and must come to self-understanding. This crisis is part of your story and one day, like me, you must share your story if it will help someone else.

Don't forget that there is tremendous power in asking for help. When you ask, assistance will always find its way to you and not always in the way you expect. Keep your eyes, ears, and sense of possibility open. You might receive a message through plants, animals, or a song that you hear while driving. You might make a new friend who leads you to the right person who will offer what you need. Dreams are often a vehicle of help. You could be visited by a relative who has gone on but returns in a dream to help you. What you need, or even what you needed that you didn't know you needed, shows up exactly in time though it may not be as expected.

My family is related to big cats. We are from the *Kaccv,* or Big Cat Clan, through my father. There is a big cat who shows up in my dreams. This cat is a barometer of my state of mind. When he walks through full of confidence and muscular acuity, I know I am on the right path. When he appears emaciated, then I need to pay acute attention to what is going on. I can call on him for help.

If nothing is getting through, and these words cannot make it through the walls of despair, then please call a suicide or help line, speak to a teacher, a friend, and don't worry about sounding stupid or feeling like you're just making it up. Do this anyway if you are anywhere near that stepping off place, if you are even thinking of it. When I walked across campus to the counseling center, I did not find the answer I needed, but going there set into motion the help I needed to live a life not driven or destroyed by fear.

You will make it through the story. Your story is timeless and was constructed by the bravery of everyone it took to get you here. With the tool of poetry you can speak to despair, you can tell off bullies, you can build a house of beauty for your spirit to live in, to rest or make a home. Other poems and songs will inspire you. Reach out to someone else to help them, as I am reaching out to help you, because someone reached out to me, all the way back through the story.

27 Addiction

You are my niece, grandchild, aunt, or friend, or a young woman I have met along the way during my travels. I watch your story on social media, hear it from concerned friends and relatives, and see you less and less. You are drinking, overdoing it on the smoke, can't let go of the emotional pain relief offered artificially and temporarily by painkilling properties of drugs prescribed for muscle pain. Or the most fun you have involves drinking, smoking, or shooting something with friends. And though you can never match the high from the first hit, you can't let it go. For a while you are free, you don't feel anxiety, you might even feel joy with your friends who ride the high with you and maybe even sold it to you. When the high dissipates the lows double back.

I remember the words from an older indigenous man whose name I have forgotten. I don't remember where we were, but there were several of us questioning addiction, bemoaning the loss of family members. He was someone we respected. He wore his life well on his body and in his face.

"What it is," he said, "is that they are looking for a vision."

Maybe each of us is on a lifelong vision quest. Maybe we are all looking for that vision that will save us, a vision in which everything make sense, including senseless atrocities. I have had moments in my dreams when the edge of the dream lifts, and this life with whose eyes I am seeing realizes that we are in the dream; we are the dream.

I remember a friend I hung out and partied with when we were young. I could always have a drink or two, or a hit, and that was it. She could not stop once she had a taste of any high, not until she was blacked out or in a drug coma. Her life was eventually destroyed by her addiction. Her son is now my relative. He has few memories of her.

I want him to see her with her long dark hair just past her shoulders, her dark eyes lit up with adventure, and hear her ongoing light-hearted sarcasm that made her friends laugh. Being mixed Navajo and Mexican was difficult in those years. There was little to no mixing then. She had a hard time knowing where she belonged, rejected by both sides. She was a good friend. We cared about each other enough to share personal stories. She went through hell to be here. I understood some burdens were too heavy to bear. I want him to know how much she loved him and loves him still, no matter her early, tragic demise. He needs to know that all stories naturally will resolve to harmony, though they don't always resolve in earth time. She will greet him one day, meet him with clear, bright eyes, and he will be the baby she never leaves.

I don't always have the words to help you, or anyone, overcome addiction. And maybe like you, I only have questions, tears, and anger. Keep in mind that some questions can pry open a corner where light can shoot through, and we can momentarily see the whole story.

28 Judgment

Once in Albuquerque I was walking down the sidewalk after leaving the university campus where I had been a student and was now teaching. Coming in my direction up the sidewalk was a group of homeless Native men. Their addiction to drink had landed them in raggy clothes with a desperate need to feed their high. I knew they would ask me for money, and I didn't like to give money to help those begging buy more drugs or alcohol. As I was about to pass them on the sidewalk I tried to pretend I was invisible, tried not to look at them, to give them any encouragement at all. Then someone in the group called out my name. I looked up. He was one of my friends from my time as a student. I knew others in the group too. We all hugged. I noticed lice thick in their hair, and odor from lack of cleanliness. We stood there on the sidewalk, a circle once again as we had been, and joked and laughed just like we used to as students. Of course I gave them money.

That night as I mulled over the encounter, I was given to this thought. Maybe these men were street warriors. They were gaining knowledge about what it means to lose everything to addiction. They had lost their homes, their family members, and themselves in this journey. Next, they would have to find their way back by finding themselves once again. It would not be easy and some of them would appear never to find home again as their bodies would be discovered frozen, run over on the railroad tracks, or overdosed. Some would eventually show up at the Native rehab center and be welcomed in. Others would be driven home to ceremony. All of them would find their way eventually through time. I considered that on this path they were gaining more knowledge than someone who had a safe nine-to-five life, someone who went to work, came home, ate, watched television, then went back to work again in the morning. Yet, to judge makes a story rigid and closed to any bright possibility. Even the safe person is involved in a teaching story.

29 Despair

You reached out, with a note, your hands, or your eyes. Even a head-down stance can be a reaching out. You do not know how you will go on. It's been one thing after another. You escaped home as a teen. You might have been a single mom by then, or not. You got yourself into school or a program. You worked. Then there were the parties. Then you cleaned up. Or maybe it wasn't quite that way. But when you fractured your foot while you were running and something you relied on to clear your head was gone, you started eating too much, watching reels, scrolling social media and reality shows. And then you were let go from a job you loved. It also paid the bills. It was Covid or before or after. You didn't want to take a job at a food chain but then you couldn't pay rent, so you did. You were let go. You lost your house. You lived in your car. Or maybe it wasn't quite that way. You got your degree then couldn't find a job. Your partner or husband found someone else. You don't know how to go on. Your baby has a condition, and you can't keep up the continual costs of care alone. Or you just don't know what to do with the despair. Politics has ripped your community apart. Your parents or grandparents pass away. Your cousin who was more a sister to you is missing and maybe murdered. She's the second one in your close family to go missing, ever since the pipeline people moved in. Your dream was a husband, or a wife, a partner, someone you could laugh with, love with, who loved children and adventure, and there is no one. Or it was your music taking you on tour, or your art finding an audience, or a house that was yours or even your own apartment, or room. Or you just aren't good enough and never were, according to your parents, the nuns, the preacher, or your teacher. Their words haunt you. Or someone has put something on you, and you don't have the funds to hire a medicine man, and no matter what you do you just can't get ahead. You are tempted to drink, stay high on gummies, or smoke, or fake pain for painkillers.

You reached out. All you need is one step. There is all the power in the world with that step. Marathons are won step by step, a climb to Mount Everest starts with a step, turning in another direction also begins with a step.

One day, when I was young, I was trapped, without money, without any other place to go. I started walking. I walked all over that town, the capital of the Cherokee Nation in the west. As I walked, I took in the beauty of the trees. I learned that the trees were the leaders of that small town. Fall was especially spectacular with color and even the evergreens lit up in their green. Squirrels were everywhere. The river that moved through the city was thick with watercress. There were many kinds of birds that watched with curiosity as I walked.

I walked down streets and looked at windows, at what I didn't have the money to buy. I began to dream as I walked. I had wanted to be an artist. It's all I ever wanted to be. I wanted to be able to move about in the world, to travel and create. I did not want a life in which I could not even afford to go to a laundromat, where I washed our clothes out in the bathtub with a small washboard. I promised myself that when I got out, I would never rely on anyone else for income.

The more I walked, the louder came the voice of my spirit who told me, you will get out of here, you can have the life you imagine. I began imagining, step by step, how to make the life I wanted. The changes didn't happen immediately, but they came about step by step.

We moved to Tulsa, and I worked cleaning at the hospital to support us. Step by step we returned to Santa Fe, to our arts community. With the help of the Eight Northern Indian Pueblos Talent Search I got into the university, step by step, I made the life I imagined as I walked. The trajectory wasn't straight or even. I stumbled many times, even failed, but I kept going step by step.

Let this story be a step with which you can lift yourself, to the next part of your journey. Take the next step, and then the next.

30 *Fear*

I release you, my beautiful and terrible
fear. I release you. You were my beloved
and hated twin, but now, I don't know you
as myself. I release you with all the
pain I would know at the death of
my children.

You are not my blood anymore.

I give you back to the soldiers
who burned down my home, beheaded my children,
raped and sodomized my brothers and sisters.
I give you back to those who stole the
food from our plates when we were starving.

I release you, fear, because you hold
these scenes in front of me and I was born
with eyes that can never close.

I release you
I release you

I release you
I release you

I am not afraid to be angry.
I am not afraid to rejoice.
I am not afraid to be black.
I am not afraid to be white.
I am not afraid to be hungry.
I am not afraid to be full.
I am not afraid to be hated.
I am not afraid to be loved.

to be loved, to be loved, fear.

Oh, you have choked me, but I gave you the leash.
You have gutted me but I gave you the knife.
You have devoured me, but I laid myself across the fire.

I take myself back, fear.
You are not my shadow any longer.
I won't hold you in my hands.
You can't live in my eyes, my ears, my voice
my belly, or in my heart my heart
my heart my heart

But come here, fear
I am alive and you are so afraid of dying.

I am sharing this poem because this poem has helped me, and many others, overcome fear. This poem came at a time in my life when I was gathering the pieces of my soul. I needed to walk forward in my young, shattered life, to continue with integrity. I struggled with an intense and paralyzing fear. It was a fear that kept me up at night, had me constantly checking under the bed, the windows, the door. Anyone could break into that flimsy-doored student apartment with cheap window locks. Druggies combed the student ghetto looking for easy break-ins for quick cash, stereos and other equipment they could sell or pawn, or for women. I was also haunted by specters of darkness, who as soon as I lay down to sleep would appear at the edge of consciousness to drag me away. They were mishappen, demonic figures. I fought them off, terrified, though I would just as often freeze and only my voice yelling from the underworld and breaking into the world where my children were sleeping, would free me. My voice would break the spell, and I would be safe, until the next time they appeared.

Those figures, I was to learn, were creations of fear. They were made up of negative thoughts of jealousy, envy, hatred, and all the other ills that beset us. We are each responsible for some of them. We are not always aware that our thoughts make actual forms. They also send messages and even receive them. Some creations of fear and ugliness are deliberately formed and sent out to harm by those who are skilled at such things and who choose a path of destruction. Some are personal, and some are made of history.

One night after a fight with the demonic figures, this poem, "I Give You Back," or what I call the "fear poem," came to me. When I say came to me, I sat down to write, and it wanted to be said. I needed it. In a way it is kind of a prayer. I do not associate prayer only with religion, rather I think of prayer as awareness focused toward connection and healing. Prayer belongs to everyone at any time. John Coltrane's songs were deliberate prayers to the Creator in gratitude. Every action or thought can be done deliberately as prayer. Poetry can be prayer. The fear poem is supplication, a kind of humble and urgent prayer to be released of fear.

Not long after I wrote the poem the demons came again for me. My spirit told me to speed up my resonance. Fear has a low vibrating resonance. Expression of gratitude is one way to lift resonance. I thought of how the sun turned the mountains to the east scarlet at sunset. I remembered how my father would lift me from the car when I had fallen asleep as a toddler and hold me to his chest. I could smell his Old Spice. Because my vibration lifted, the demons reaching to grab me could not touch me. They fell away and I never saw them again.

You can make your own fear poem or song, or other song that will help you overcome. Singing lifts words into other dimensions where they can move more freely.

31 *Transform*

I don't write poetry to send messages. My art is about investigating the illumination of the world, lifting the underneath of the unknown, and making a path of beauty through uncertainty and chaos. Even love poems written with potent purpose can be composed with words you will never find in popular love poems and songs, and in a manner that opens doorways to the heart that were never noticed or unlocked before with words.

I am also asked about the themes in my poetry. Transformation and the need for justice compel me to write and create.

In one of my earlier poems, I wanted to transform hatred into love in a poem.

Sunrise

Sunrise, as you enter the houses of everyone here, find us.
We've been crashing for days, or has it been years.
Find us, beneath the shadow of this yearning mountain, crying here.

We have been sick with sour longings, and the jangling of fears.
Our spirits rise up in the dark, because they hear
Doves in cottonwoods calling forth the sun.
We struggled with a monster and lost.
Our bodies were tossed in the pile of kill.
We rotted there.
We were ashamed and we told ourselves for a thousand years
We didn't deserve anything but this—
And one day, in relentless eternity, our spirits discerned
movement of prayers
Carried toward the sun.
And this morning we are able to stand with all the rest
And welcome you here.
We move with the lightness of being, and we will go
Where there's a place for us.

I see poems as transformational stations, like electrical transformers. I have learned that you can put just about anything in a poem, if it will fit and if it is necessary to the poem. I have washed my mother's body in a poem, when I was not allowed the opportunity at her death. I have stood in the stars and looked out on the earth in admiration. I have walked into the future and returned with my arms full of flowers.

32 Lost

Right now, in the story making, I am stopping to admit I don't know for sure exactly what I am doing, where I am, or how I will get there. This often happens in story making. You come to a place, a time, and nothing looks familiar. The direction isn't clearly mapped or even suggested. This is when you need to stop for a moment, sit down, take a breath or two, and bring in curiosity. Check out the scenery, test the wind for direction, taste the earth. Maybe you just need a break from the pace, and after a time away from the story, you soon find an opening, a road, a compelling character. You might need more than a moment. You might need a day, a few days, a week, month, year, or even more. Maybe that hummingbird who just flew by your head making that whirring sound with its wings shows you where you need to go. Or, with curiosity by your side, you discover there is another part of the story that never occurred before and you need more information before proceeding, so you go to the online or in-person library, or a mentor, to learn what the story demands before going forward. Maybe this wasn't the right time and place for the story.

Some stories have power only if they are told in a particular place. Some of our tribal stories are that way. To take them away from their place weakens them and can be dangerous to the one moving the story, or to those hearing it somewhere other than where it belongs. The story might not be the right story at this time, and you must walk away. Or, you write about trying to find the story, as I am doing right now.

As I sit here the hummingbird is zooming back and forth, curious as to why I am here in her story and wondering why my red watchband looks like a different kind of flower. She questions whether there is sustenance to be found on my wrist, in this moment of bright sun on this early fall day.

I watch a jumping spider who has claimed this studio house as her domain. There has been no one here for a while to disturb her, so she has been very busy. She has covered the whole border of the back door with her webbing. Even the porch light is decorated and the area around the light. She has been weaving to make houses for her children, and to catch the food they need because the light attracts prey. She is now watching me, noting that I am moving around too much to weave me into her art. Story making is like weaving.

I remember Leslie Silko and her story making and how she told the story of the girl being rolled down the hill in an outhouse after being caught in an indiscretion. My friend from Paguate and I laughed and laughed at Leslie's telling. My baby girl Rainy Dawn toddled around us as we listened on Leslie's front porch at Old Laguna.

Silko reminded readers many times in her novels and short stories that we are part of a web of imagination, that even as we are weaving our own tales, we are also being woven into a dynamic story that leaps from generation to generation, across cultures, landscapes, and time.

Stories like to be fed. You can feed them with thoughts, dreams, even nightmares, and gossip. They in turn nourish you or can addict you. Our cultures are essentially stories, songs, movement, and images.

Your first cry opens the earth door
You join the ancestor road
With your pack of stories
Slung on your back
You venture into the spiral
Of creation and destruction
You are them
They are you
You make more—

We are compelled to make stories to assist in finding the way through mythic or ordinary times. They remind us that sometimes we must stop, go around, through time, under, inside, or to the outside where nothing familiar is known. And sometimes we're in an outhouse when it happens, being rolled down the hill. It depends on how you make the weave. You can even sing the weave. Listen close. It might be singing you.

33 Dreaming

On average, I learned, we dream two or three hours a night. When I was young, I began writing dreams down. Dreams can be some of your most profound teachers. I found that some were anxiety dreams: they expressed fears and concerns. Some dreams were from eating or drinking too much before sleep. Some dreams were visitations of those who had passed before. You could meet up with them and visit and sometimes they brought messages.

Once in a dream, a beloved aunt came to me, shortly after she had passed. She came to me very upset. She had left a will. The aunt in charge of the dispensation of her property had ignored her will, had sold everything for almost nothing, and kept the proceeds.

Some dreams were in super reality. I was awake in them. In those dreams I was usually shown or given something powerful to ponder, to bring back.

One dream came to me as I was near the end of the story making for a memoir. It was one of those dreams that stood apart because it carried light. I saw myself at the doorway of time. I was holding a child of the seventh generation in my arms. I adjusted the blanket to see her face, to see what this one was bringing with her to share. It is in the manner that I had taken every child, grandchild, and great-grandchild into my arms to welcome them, to bless them during my time walking on the earth. I smiled at this girl who looked at me with her eyes that shone with the memory of the place she was coming from, and with hope for the story she would make here.

I sang into the baby a song that would give her strength, and sustenance, a song that would call her ancestors to stand behind her, no matter the trials, no matter history and heartbreak. Then I walked with her into time and delivered the baby to the earth story that needed her.

Maybe one day I will write a book of dreams, not as if they were dreams, but as if they are happening, for they are happening in the story-making reality.

Recently when the dreams started appearing in short fragments, like reels and TikTok videos and not in their long-legged mythic shapes, I knew I had engaged too much with such platforms. In those forms, there is no profound unfolding of metaphorical revelation. Because I didn't want empty, fast clips of dream stuff, I turned off Reels and Tik Tok to save my dreaming.

34 *Alert*

Some years ago, I flew into Newark for a performance and school visit at a college in New Jersey. I unfolded my itinerary to see where I was going. I read the name of the college. It was in a small town I had never heard of before. I noted it was nearly midnight and I had an early class visit. I had just flown across the country and was tired.

I asked the driver from the car service where we were headed. He responded, "The last stop on the New Jersey Turnpike." When I heard those words, I got that weird feeling I get when I know that something is going to unfold for which I need to stay on alert. We each have an internal awareness system that gives warning. Sometimes it feels like the yellow of a caution light. Other times it is a full-on flashing red and then you know you must pay immediate attention, stop, get out, and run.

One morning when I was headed out to paddle with our canoe club, I had one of those flashing red warnings. I had just been placed in a canoe and we headed out into the bay. The water felt uneasy. There was a storm coming in. We got caught in wave action, the canoe turned over, and we couldn't right it. As we held on to the keel of the upside-down canoe, I made the decision that I would swim in if I had to. All of us crew were about to start swimming when a small fishing boat rescued us.

As we neared the last exit on the New Jersey Turnpike, the driver asked me to help him find the hotel. He hadn't been able to see it clearly because the hotel sign was dim. As we drove up, we questioned whether the hotel was open. The office was dark, and the reception area was covered with drop cloths. The cash register was on a card table. A night clerk came out of an office door to check me in, assuring us that they were open. The driver reluctantly left me there.

The clerk handed me a key and directed me to the elevators. The door to my floor opened to a crisscrossing of masking tape and a sign: DO NOT ENTER. I pushed my way through the tape. I wasn't about to walk the stairs with my bags. I walked up and down every corridor on that floor, key in my hand, looking for my room number. There was no room number matching my key number. I crossed back through the barrier into the elevator, bags and all, and returned to the makeshift front desk. I noted the large construction equipment lining the hallways and knew I wouldn't get much sleep. The clerk looked at my key and said, "Oh, that room has no number above the door." I asked for a different room, preferably one I could find. There were no other rooms, she said. She directed me to another hotel down the turnpike.

By then it was very early in the morning. I could see the other hotel in the distance, but it meant walking the turnpike with my bags. As girls and women, we are aware of the danger of strangers, of men who could accost or steal us, from the time we can walk. This could happen at night or in bright daylight.

I still shiver over the story of a granddaughter who was walking home from the school bus stop just a few blocks from home, when a stranger tried to force her into his car. She remembered the warnings and darted from the predator. She made it home. We are in a national epidemic of those who never make it home and are never heard from again. It's important to pay attention as it might save your life.

As I walked the turnpike, I sent my senses ahead of me on high alert and asked for protection. We can do that at any time, anywhere. I felt a line of safety leading me to the hotel I could see in the distance. If I had sensed otherwise, I would have turned around and returned to the first hotel, maybe even called a taxi even though I doubted there were taxis available at that hour. I trust my inner alert system. It has always been right.

As I set out, I grounded myself deeply in my surroundings. I made friends with the trees and bushes along the way, noting who they were and thanking them for the hard job they were doing cleaning the air, as they perched there at the edge of a freeway where thousands of vehicles zoomed by daily. I covered myself with the blanket of stars overhead. They could see the whole story, even into past and future time. It felt so good to be outside after being on airplanes all day. And then what helped was laughing to myself about what a story this would make one day.

I made it to the alternate hotel and soon learned that the story hadn't ended. There was no dark, drop-clothed check-in desk here. I set my bags down in my room, but here I was again in that weird feeling. My now wide-open senses felt an oppressiveness that was so heavy I could hardly breathe. There was something in that room. I sat there hoping that feeling would go away if I just gave it time. Finally, I walked with my bags back down to the front desk and changed rooms. There was such a difference in atmosphere I knew that I hadn't imagined anything.

The next morning as I checked out, I asked the clerk about the first room. She exclaimed, "I can't believe she put you in that room. Someone died of pneumonia in there and we have never been able to get rid of the feeling or that smell. We don't usually rent out that room."

I drank a lot of coffee that morning, and I am rarely a coffee drinker. And I made it to my engagements, bearing a new story about that time I had to walk along the New Jersey Turnpike in the middle of the night.

35 Forgiveness

One of my teachers asked me to assist her with a healing ceremony to help participants forgive and release those who had harmed them, to free themselves. As I stood next to her, assisting her, I could see as she saw. Behind every workshop participant stood someone. Some participants even had a line. Around each participant was an emotional field full of mixtures of regret, anger, sadness, and any other concern that needed to be cleared for forgiveness.

The teacher unwound a length of ribbon. She held the center, while each participant took a length and returned a length to the teacher, who was the spoke at the center of the circle. The teacher lifted words for release, for forgiveness, then I passed the scissors so each person could cut the cord that was keeping them bound to the pain of the burden of the story. As every ribbon was cut the room grew lighter and lighter as everyone in the circle was set free.

36 In Our Hands

I was told by a South Indian astrologer that you can heal with your eyes. I believe this to be so. We communicate almost everything with our eyes, also with our gestures, our speech, and our hands. Healing is something our bodies know how to do innately. We share healing with others just as we can share discord, and who's to say in the long run that discord isn't part of the healing.

In my late twenties I had a friend who was suffering from a plantar wart. They appear on the bottom of your feet and grow inward. They can cause pain. She was having trouble walking.

When I was a child the adults used to like me to massage their backs and sometimes even walk on them. I asked her if I could take her foot in my hands. I wanted to give relief. As I massaged, I breathed love into the foot and the area of the plantar wart. I don't know how I knew to do this except that it was what I was led to do as a child. Within the next few weeks, the plantar wart disappeared.

I was a helper. Her body took what it needed to heal.

We can all do this for each other. We all have hands that can heal. Our eyes can heal. These words I am writing can heal, as can yours.

37 Witness

Our generations are different in what and how we witness. My generation was the first to watch war playing out in our homes on the evening news. We watched a president be killed in a motorcade in our living rooms. Now local, national, and global events take place constantly on the small screens of our computers, cell phones, and other devices. We witness starvation, massacres, and other massive cruelties, even as we witness local, national, and global sports triumphs and other stories all on screens that reach us in our homes and as we travel. We carry these devices with us, and even wear them.

We used to trust the source of the stories that appeared on national news, though we were always aware that the slant of the stories and what was chosen for us to see and hear was based on biases and the ownership of the news source. Still, for the most part there were standards of journalism. Now we don't know the story sources and we cannot trust who or what to believe. False stories can be constructed by insurgent forces within and without our borders to interfere with politics and economics. We are left with the need to evaluate the hundreds, even thousands of stories that cross into our homes, our ears, our eyes. What do we do with all those stories, and the effects of all those stories on us, when the average person scrolls eighty-eight miles a year? Once we have seen these images, heard these stories, then we are witness. What do we do with the emotional weight of it, and how do we discern the truth?

Some years ago, before the overtake of the internet, a young granddaughter told me that the angels used to come and talk to her every night. But since she had to share a room with her older sister they weren't showing up as much. They told her that her sister's computer, as it played music or movies, made it more difficult for them to speak to her.

Turn off your computer, quiet your cell phone, shut down your other devices. Go out into the real world of dirt, leaf, wind, of sunlight and rain. Take one day a week, or a whole week, or more to clean your ears. Limit manufactured stories. Go to trusted sources. Take up a particular story or cause and enact change. Give back in some way to the community. Always question the veracity of any story, its source and intent. Pay attention to what stories you are creating. And maybe the angels will return to speak to you.

38 Historical Trauma

When I was coming up my generation had never heard the term "historical trauma." Yet the term is now ubiquitous in our Native communities, as we continue to work through the wounding from genocidal acts against Native peoples perpetrated for the last few centuries throughout this whole western hemisphere. Perhaps we need to add the phrase "historical empowerment" and remember that we have come through an unprecedented era in the timeless history of our peoples in which we have been profoundly tested by genocidal acts to destroy us. Not only have we survived but we have continued our cultures and languages, we've continued to carry our original values, embody our selfhood as Native Nations.

When you are born, time is endless. In early childhood a day lasts forever. And then as you age time appears to run faster and faster. When you are elderly, a day happens in a snap of time. Then consider the expanse of all time, eternal time, and how each indigenous nation exists within that sweep of memory. When you keep in mind that immensity of timelessness, then the centuries of colonization are relatively short. We need to remember to see ourselves as Native nations as much more expansive in presence than in the short measure of colonization. We were here, we are here now and will be here long after colonization has destroyed itself from the inside.

Historical trauma and empowerment have been in the conversations lately of my circle of Native mothers, grandmothers, and great-grandmothers. This morning when I checked in with my friend, the Eastern Band Cherokee attorney Brenda Pipestem, I told her I was at work on a book to pass on some of the stories I have gathered from ancestors and mentors. She told me, as she spoke from her home community of EBC in North Carolina, "Tell them that their mothers are still dealing with historical trauma, and for them to work out what they can before having children. Start healing themselves so that their children don't carry it on."

I can hear what my youthful response to this would have been: *They should carry their own trauma. I have my own life to live.*

Counter to the Indian school stories of previous centuries, I ran away to Indian school to save my life. I ran to the community of other Native students, all of us artists at a Native art school. We all carried historical trauma. We used the torque of history to make beauty, to save ourselves and our families. When it worked, my generation found our way through the story of our time. When it didn't, we faltered and lost ourselves.

Trauma can also erupt from intentional personal misuses or mistakes, or even from unintentional acts, like disturbing animals, plants, or places on the land.

One night I was up worrying over a problem. I bent close in curiosity to the story, to figure out the pulse, what it was doing to me and how I could get rid of it and/or alleviate the pain. I saw that it had not originated from me. It was my mother's. She hadn't cleared it in her lifetime. I then symbolically cut the cord so it would not pass on to the children, grandchildren, or great-grandchildren to inherit it. I asked for assistance to transform it.

As I speak, I can feel the prayers of ancestors reaching down to us to help us as we navigate these times, these challenges. They give encouragement. I can see them nodding their heads in affirmation to Brenda's caution and looking on with tenderness as we continue to find our way through times that are very different, yet not so different at all.

A caution here: some ancestors are troublemakers. They always were and they are still at it.

39 *Missing*

You might live your whole life looking for justice and never find it. What justice will ever return a murdered daughter to her mother? What justice will ever relieve the suffering of our daughters and sons stolen from our arms, our homes, our families, then and now? How do we find her, find them, and bring them home? How do we change a system that makes it acceptable for our daughters and our sons to be stolen, sexually and violently abused? How do we bring justice to right the legal theft of minerals, resources, and lands? How do we ensure the rights of women to oversee our own bodies, our own communities? How do we bring justice to mothers and fathers who are grieving their children and the future of their children?

How will we ever bring history to justice?

I am asking you, this next generation who are making a story that will address questions of injustice in our country, our communities, our homes, and our families.

One of the teachers of hoʻoponopono, Dr. Ihaleakala Hew Len, used this Hawaiian method of making things right to empty out an asylum in Hawaiʻi. When he arrived, the institution was in chaos. Patients were fighting each other and the staff. He was very calm and assured. He would look at their charts and walk through the ward. Soon those who had been considered incurable and beyond help were walking out the doors of the asylum. At the end of his four years there, there were no more patients. When asked what he had done he said, "I was healing the part of me that created them."

He believed that everything in your life is your life. Each patient was his life, and he assisted in healing them from within.

Imagine this being done with history.

Don't ever give up looking for those who are missing, or helping restore that which has been lost or forgotten that remains essential to our well-being.

40 Orientation

I remember standing in the street in Anchorage one January morning. It was cold and dark. Even though it was already ten in the morning, the sun was just edging the horizon. I try to remember to face east every morning and greet the rising sun, wherever I am on earth. When the sun crosses the horizon, it makes for potent energy. We can breathe it, hold it in our hands, then send it out with our breath, words, and songs to assist others.

One's relationship with the sun is essential to the shape of our Mvskoke belief system. The sun is a relative. We honor the presence and gift of light brought by Sun to all who live here on the planet, a presence we call Mother Earth in English. That light is *vnokeckv* moving through all things. It is the fire within our fire, and without it we would not be.

As I stood far from home, I realized that my culture wouldn't fit in this place at all. Because of the sun's angle, and the resultant climate there, the plants were different and had different seasons, the animals were also different, and so were the elements and all that we need for our lives. Even our songs, our clothes, our designs fit themselves to the land and how the light moves about the land. How we are placed in the circle of the globe, the circle of this solar system, the galactic system, and beyond defines every particular of our human cultural experience.

What happens with changing climate will enact change in every aspect of our lives. Years ago, prophecies told us that one day the sun would not be as bright, and when that happened, we would begin to see drastic effects of climate change. My generation has watched the sun lose its brightness with the air pollution that intensified with population explosion, exploitation of resources like fossil fuels, and greed.

When the Arctic melts, polar bears no longer have a home, nor can the caribou follow their migration paths. Cultures that have crucial relationships with polar bears, with caribou, with the plant life that sustains the animals, including two-legged humans, are forced to change. Not only is the polar ice melting, but the Amazon greenbelt is also being burned to a fraction of its former reach. With climate change, shorelines are shifting, and some lands are disappearing. When you lose your indigenous lands, you are in danger of losing your culture.

Here on our reservation, we are watching climate change affect our ceremonial times. First it was cultural change that shifted our new year from being close to a particular new moon, to being timed to coincide with the work week schedule. Now the unusually warm summer temperatures send us into later summer for the occurrence of the new year.

If it is in the nature of stories to resolve to harmony, then one day we will once again understand our relationship to the sun and how we interact with the elements and they with us. We will know again that we are the earth.

41 Greeter

One night marked a medical crisis for my stepsister, who was in the intensive care unit in the hospital. We were warned that that night marked a crucial crossroads: she would either make it, or not. With that news, I stayed up until late with prayers for her recovery, for her journey. None of us knew which direction her story would take. The next morning, I was relieved to learn that she had survived. She called me about a week later with a story.

> *I found myself in the dark and could sense others nearby. I saw others ahead of me walking the road to a brilliant light. The light was like the sun, but brighter than the sun, yet you could look at it and it wouldn't hurt your eyes. Then suddenly next to me was my favorite cat, Clyde!! I shouldn't say favorite because I have loved all my cats. Clyde must have known how much I was missing him. He had passed of old age recently and I was still mourning him, still startled not to find him in his favorite lounging spots where he liked to lounge and drink in sun. I told Clyde how happy I was to see him, and how much we all*

missed him. It just wasn't the same without him around. Clyde told me he missed me too. As I think about it, it didn't even strike me as weird that he spoke to me. We always had our own language. He was my soulmate, that is besides my husband; he was my cat soulmate.

We walked side by side along the road, drawn toward the light. Now I know what moths experience as they are compelled to the porchlight. You don't even think about it. It's instinct beyond thought. I filled Clyde in on all the goings on, what the kids and grandkids were up to— I told him about my grandson who was afraid of monsters in his room. He was a lot like me when I was young, I told him, extra sensitive. We were getting closer and closer to the light. I knew somehow that if I stepped into the aura of that light, there would be no turning back to the story that I had made so far of my life. I told Clyde I had to go back. I couldn't leave my husband, especially not now. He needed me. I told Clyde that I wanted more time with my children, my grandchildren, and what about the cats who were still there at home, waiting for me?

Clyde nodded his head wisely. I was beginning to understand that he existed in timelessness, which was so like the experience of catness, in whatever realm of existence. Clyde could see, hear, and feel beyond human sense. Clyde told me he understood and would be waiting there again for me when it was time for me to return.

And then, she said, I turned around to come back and woke up in the hospital room just as dawn was coming through the window.

She told me she no longer feared death because she knew Clyde would be there. She called me to tell me because she knew I would believe her story.

I did and I do.

And I wanted to write it down to give it to her grandson, who is now grown, so he will know that the story continues, because I sensed that she told me the story to pass it along to him so he would have it when he needed it. The story was also something she left behind, to give to you, so you would no longer be afraid of dying.

42 Butterfly

I returned home to the reservation for a visit after being gone for years, living mostly in New Mexico and other areas of the Southwest, Los Angeles, and Hawai'i. Like any Native person close to community, you always come home, but visiting is different than the everyday experience of living rooted in traditional community. The one who returns can be viewed with suspicion as we often bring unwelcome influences or are no longer fluent in traditions. It can be awkward for everyone, but in the end the circle is your family.

Joyce welcomed me to her camp, a shelter for cooking and visiting, which was two down from the camp where I helped cook. She was from Paguate, a Laguna Pueblo village, and had married in with our people. Because I had lived for years in New Mexico, I knew many of her people and was familiar with their cultural traditions, so we had a common place of understanding. Who else could say "down the line" and know what it meant or know of the various kinds of chiles and food specialties and how to cook them.

Our friendship mattered and I always looked forward to seeing her and her family. She had some health issues, then one day she was dying. I had gotten the word and could feel her slipping away. I went into prayer space, which is a kind of field between the now and no time. As I prayed for her, I saw her spirit and sensed her awareness of me. There were many others whose prayers surrounded her and made for a lightness of being as she was beginning to step from this realm into the forever realm. That night, she was gone.

My husband and I were living then above the Tennessee River in Knoxville. We often walked the perimeter of the condo grounds, a place that had been an overlook for Mvskoke people and had once been a Civil War camp. There were many trees and plants, including blueberry shrubs, and many animals also lived there, such as turkeys and groundhogs.

As we began our walk the morning after our friend passed, a black butterfly caught our attention. It circled us and made designs in the air in front of us. The butterfly was very noticeable and beautiful with the black sheen of her wings contrasting with electric blue. We had never seen such a butterfly up there or witnessed such a dance. I wondered aloud if that butterfly was Joyce, giving us a message, especially as the butterflies are a major motif in Pueblo cultures, as they are associated with plants and rain.

Butterfly followed us for a while, as we took in the morning, circling and dancing around us. Then our attention fell away as we were taken in by other details emerging along our walk: someone moving out, manager gossip, and wondering about the proposed improvements that we would have to vote on.

When we returned to our condo after our walk, as I waited for my husband to unlock the front door, I was directed by instinct to look down. On the ground between my feet, perfectly placed, was a black butterfly. I heard the message, "Yes, that was me. I have made it home. I wanted you to know."

We are in mystery, ever moving, ever changing.

43 Grief

You will be broken with grief at least once in this life, maybe even a hundred times over, and you will never know the shape of it. You might know how it begins but you will never know how it ends, or if it ends at all.

"Once upon a time" I lost someone not possible to lose. Not in my lifetime and not before me. It was unimaginable, this loss. We were one, she and I. She was my laughter, my joy. We made it through the rough waters of her transformation from childhood to warrior. When I foresaw the challenges of that transformation during her coming of age, I wrote this poem to make a place, a haven to assist us in making it through the story. I recalled her birth:

I can still close my eyes and open them four floors up
looking south and west from the hospital
the approximate direction of Acoma—
and farther on to the roofs of the houses of the gods who have learned
there are no endings, only beginnings.
That day so hot, heat danced in waves off bright car tops, we both
stood poised at that door from the east, listened for a long time

to the sound of our grandmothers' voices
the brushing wind of sacred wings, the rattle of
rain drops in dry gourds.
I had to participate in the dreaming of you into memory,
cupped your head in the bowl of my body
as ancestors lined up to give you a name made of their dreams cast once more
into this stew of precious spirit and flesh.
And let you go, as I am letting you go once more in this ceremony
of the living.
And when you were born, I held you wet and unfolding,
like a butterfly newly born from the chrysalis of my body.
And breathed with you as you breathed your first breath.
Then was your promise to take it on like the rest of us,
this immense journey, for love, for rain.

She brought forth beautiful children and art, despite the tremendous struggle of everyday living. She never wanted me to see her pain, her challenge, as she counted it as weakness. Where she saw weakness, I saw strength.

Then she was gone, this gift of her, returned to her origin place to bring rain where rain is needed.

I now know of what grief is made, I know what grief smells like, how it lingers, how it won't let go, how it fractures what you imagined the world to be. That world is no longer. I was told not to look for her, to let her go, for tears bind the spirit to earth. Yet I must know that she is safe, to know she made it home.

Then in a dream, within weeks after her departure, I was sitting on a hill with a Pueblo friend of mine. Together we saw a light figure come dancing from the sky. She was shimmering like a rainbow. She danced about us, much in the way a butterfly flits and arcs through wind. It was her. I was happy. She was happy. We were all happy. Then she bent close to me, careful not to touch earth. She told me, "Look outside," then she disappeared. I woke up and looked at the weather app on my phone. It was snowing in Albuquerque. In Pueblo cosmology, those who go before bring rain and snow.

We who are left behind falter in our cloudy dreams
It's hard to let go of anything.
And what to do with all this grief.
Now there's a new story born. It's how she found wings.
Now she can do everything.

44 Compassion

In my youth we had what we called "slam books." Each page bore the name of a student or friend. Below it we would write what we thought of them. These books made the rounds of the hallways and classrooms, from girl to girl. The comments were usually praise or silly commentary, but comments could get ugly, even mean.

Now we have the internet and social media. It can resemble a large slam book in which the whole world has access to comments and images. False stories and gossip can easily be constructed and distributed. Once they are posted there is no catching them. Even someone's facial image can be placed over a nude body and made to say or do anything. This happens frequently to young women.

We also played the game Telephone. One person whispered a phrase to the next person in line, and then the next and the next. Then we compared what the last person captured with the original words. It was never the same. The difference was often shocking.

A story began making the rounds in a corner of my family. The betrayal against me was so heartbreaking that in my walk to the river to pray for healing I stumbled and fractured my feet. I couldn't run from the story now. I had to figure out what I was going to do with a story that was so damaging it caused physical harm. I had to find some way to disarm it so it could no longer hurt me. I had to accept that the maker of the story was the same person who would in the past have come to me to help heal the disruption in our family.

In times like this I missed living near the Pacific Ocean. When the unbearable surfaced I could load up my outrigger canoe and head to the beach. I would paddle out, dive off the canoe into the salty waters of renewal. Those waters cleaned off negativity. I needed those waters now. That was one of many gifts and lessons of the Pacific. The waters also taught me that if you fought the water, or the story, you would go down. I had fought the story, and I had gone down.

And what if the story was unfolding exactly as it should? What if it was necessary that each of us go through our various roles and versions of stories to gain understanding, to even stand up and slay the monster-story, confront the story maker to learn courage? My mentors had taught that everyone was a beloved person and loved equally by the Creator. Everyone is here to learn, to be creative with the materials and elements of a life given to them with which to make a story. Everyone is tested. We will all stumble.

I was in deep mourning not just for my daughter, but for family, for our life all together that up until that rip in the story had been full of laughter and loving.

My thoughts were like flies attracted to the wounding. It was my thoughts that were now hurting me and no one else. Normally I would write it all out as I have always done, but I could not write anything. I had not been able to write anything for months, because of my grief. There appeared to be no beginning or end to any of it.

I was in a hotel room in Arizona when the betrayal thought-loop that had continued to spin and spin inside my head stopped. With prayer my thoughts became the agave plants that lined the walk along the way to the conference hall. My thoughts were the tall saguaros that guarded the compound of rooms. They were the shifting blue, blue skies above us. The haunting had no hold against beauty. I was told that we are all part of one large story, no matter what it might look like in earth time and place.

We cannot change anyone; we can only shift how we will respond to what challenges us in the stories we walk through and participate in. We are here to assist each other with whatever was gifted to us to share, to build each other up, and are not to deliberately cause harm or destroy each other.

Though I missed that relative and believe in the love that once connected us, I refused to harden myself as I walked with strength, into the opposite direction of betrayal.

45 *Flower*

My African violet plant was dying. She had been with me for more than a few years, hanging with me through more than one residence. She had bloomed consistently through the whole time we had been together. Then I left on a trip and forgot to leave the specific directions for watering her. She was overwatered. By the time I returned, her roots had begun rotting. We had communicated every morning as I opened the blinds in her corner of the world and gave encouragement for her to heal. Before long there were no flowers, and the leaves that would push their way into the world were small and atrophied. As I tried to save her, she also tried saving herself. This went on for a few months. I kept asking her where her flowers were because I missed them. She had been so generous with her flowers. One morning there was one tiny purple flower. That was her final gift to me. Within a few weeks she was gone.

46 *Coming of Age*

We see you, with your mother earthiness shooting through your youth with such fierceness, such urgency. If you could see yourselves the way that we, who were you once in our lives, see you, you would be amazed at your power, the magic you can spin, the beauty that you are so quick to question.

If these words could do anything, they would enable you to embrace your wild imagination, honor your femaleness, and remind yourself of your birthright of bravery as you step into your given life with no hesitation due to fear or shame.

In many of our indigenous cultures, and in cultures around the world, our communities make a special place for this time in your life. Our Mvskoke people traditionally honored women and the roles women play in life at the becoming of womanhood. In our traditional culture we did not demean girls, women, and female bodies. We did not assign worth based on a belief in the superiority of males, ownership of property, and an imposed hierarchy of value in which women, or female power, were disregarded and held at the bottom of a scale of worth. To do so makes no common sense.

There would be no children without women to bear, carry, and raise them. The ownership of property is not the measure of the spirit of a man or anyone else. The need to acquire is seen as a sickness. We need the balance of male and female energies, and to honor the place each of us has in this circle of becoming.

What marks the beginning of your coming of age is the beginning of your bleeding. This is when you are embraced by female relatives for the teachings you need and the gifts you would need to make a good life. At that time, if you were Mvskoke, eight mentors would come to your house to instruct you. The first would be someone who could see your story and would pass on wisdom for you to make the best decisions. Second, a medicine woman who could diagnose illness. Third, an herbalist who would teach the identification, care, and use of plants. Fourth, a "voice controller," someone who would help you develop the full range of your voice for all the functions you would take part in, including cheering, mourning, and speaking. Fifth would be a teacher of tribal civics, who would teach ethics and how to maneuver through the many connections of clans and family networks. Sixth would be a teacher of songs, to teach you the repertoire you would need to know to fully participate as a community member. Seventh, an animal tracker. And finally, eighth, to teach you a mother's role, that is, how to mother that which is needed for the survival of a people. This can be our own children, the children of others, and what we need to know of culture to pass on to others.

What if we reinstated these mentors in contemporary times? They would be very similar; for instance, learning animal tracking and the properties and uses of herbs is still useful. The Navajo Nation requires its princesses, who are designated as a kind of coming-of-age position, to be able to butcher a sheep. Someone who could help you as you begin to form your story, someone who could foresee some of the challenges you might face, could be very helpful. A physical exam can always be useful, especially one that accesses not just bodily conditions, but mental, emotional, and spiritual conditions as well. What strikes me as important, but is not usually considered, is being taught to use your voice. To be able to use your voice well is empowerment. Knowing how to use your voice can make a difference in how you are perceived and help you assert your power in many different situations. We could all use lessons in ethics, even how to assert ethics. Learning songs and music develops parts of you that are untouched by other modes of learning. I would include learning your family's indigenous language with learning songs, but that is assumed in traditional ways.

Your Mvskoke relatives would gather and collect twenty-eight gifts to give you. A few of them are a personal cup, spoon, bed mat and covers, and three buckets: one for clear water, one for herbal water, and one for specific herbal baths. You would also receive a chair, hairbrush, a new set of clothes, a medicine bag, and baskets of different sizes, among other gifts. This is a celebration of you, and how you are part of a family who is collectively recognizing your worth. The blowing of a conch shell would mark the opening and closing of this meeting to honor you and show you the way.

This gift giving could be easily adapted and still fit these times. These items are all useful; think about how you would value each one, knowing that a relative had chosen something particular for you, especially for this time.

Each young woman, just like each young man, should be accompanied to the doorway of adulthood and be given blessings and the gifts they need to begin a successful path in life.

Let's all step into the circle of this story and consider how we can work together to see girls becoming through the story. We can begin here, and now.

Our relatives in that beloved place dressed you in black hair,
Brown eyes, skin the color of earth, and turned you in this direction.
We want you to know that we urgently gathered to welcome you here; we came
Bearing gifts to celebrate:

From your mother's house we brought poetry, music, medicine makers,
stubbornness, beauty, tribal leaders, a yard filled with junked cars and
the gift of knowing how to make them run.
We carried tobacco and cedar, new clothes and joy for you.
And from your father's house came educators, thinkers, dreamers,
weavers and mathematical genius.
They carried a cradleboard, hope, white shell and turquoise for you.
We brought blankets to wrap you in, soft beaded moccasins of deerskin.

Did you hear us as you traveled from your rainbow house?
We called you with thunder, with singing.
Did you see us as we gathered in the town beneath the mountains?
We were dressed in concern and happiness. . . .

Now, breathe.
And when you breathe remember the source of the gift of all breathing.
When you walk, remember the source of the gift of all walking.
And when you run, remember the source of the gift of all running.
And when you laugh, remember the source of the gift of all laughter.
And when you cry, remember the source of the gift of all tears.
And when you dream, remember the source of the gift of all dreaming.
And when your heart is broken, remember the source of the gift of
all breaking.
And when your heart is put back together, remember the source of all
putting back together. . . .

Always within you is that day your spirit came to us . . .
And you are here to bless.

47 *Passion*

I always remember the story the Anishinaabe novelist Louise Erdrich told of the woman whose lover lived in the bottom of the lake. When the woman would go visit him, she would put on her best clothes then walk into the lake. Eventually you would only see her hat bobbing along the surface of the water, then a small swirl of a wake as she disappeared to meet him. At dusk she would return to her children.

When I imagine her, I see her as older, not a young woman taken away by passion, but an older woman whose passions have been tempered by time, but are still burning, the way a wood fire is mostly embers in the early hours of the morning, after burning all night, much hotter than a young fire. She is fine living in her own house, which is exactly how she likes it, and she has no notion to become water.

This story might seem the fantasy of a fiction writer. This wasn't just a story, Erdrich reminded her listeners. The community knew that woman and still talked about her. She's gone now but the story of her remains. It's an old story of how a passionate love, in which your fire is matched by the fire of another, can take you into realms you would never have entered alone. The urgency to connect burns in all of us. For some it burns low, and others are overtaken by it.

When we first take on breath, the ember of life is lit in us. It represents our motivation to live, to create, to bring life into being, and gives impetus to battle the monsters of challenges. At the transformational time of adolescence, the flame is powered up by the shift in the body's hormones. It tries to find stability as it establishes itself at the level required by adulthood. It can burn wild and even appear uncontrollable. It burns throughout your life. I'm convinced this life force exists even in those life forms we call mythic.

Perhaps it is passion of one sort or another that compels people to change form, pursue an impossible liaison or accomplishment, and to imagine and thereby create creatures like dragons or tie snakes.

Unusual things can happen at the intersection of time, form, and place when high passion is motivating fire.

I understand that woman who walks into the water to meet her lover once a week. She is carrying a living fire, a fierce need. She is transformed and has been transformed by love. Though she is an earth person, she descends into water, to a lover who is a water being.

In another version she is younger. She is forced to reckon how she will go forward with this love. She can either turn her back on her earth people to live with her water lover or bring him to land to live with her. There is no in-between for her as her fire burns and burns. Either their story would be a warning to the people, or their union would bring gifts for the people.

There are transformational moments at every age. There is one every seven years, a renewal. Don't forget, as you move through the changes, that you carry fire. It will brighten; it will dim. It can consume you and destroy you. It can also light the way.

48 Resonance

Every place has a signature energy, as does every object, every being. What someone has made or held, or anything material, carries the story of how it was made, where it has been, how it has been used. If there were a way you could unwind the story embedded in a piece of pottery, you could hear the conversations had while the pot was being built or thrown. Imagine what you could hear if you could unwind the energy of a piece of pottery from hundreds of years ago. When traveling you can especially notice this—how every city, every community has a story, a history, a certain *feel* about it.

On a trip to Peru a few years back, the first stop on the way to Machu Picchu was the old city of Cusco, more than eleven thousand feet high in the Andes Mountains. It is an ancient city, the capital of the Incan empire, tucked in lands layered with centuries of indigenous presence and thought. While in the city I visited the Museo Inka, to get a sense of the ancestral story of the original peoples there. The tour guide was informative as we walked through the rooms showcasing ancient Incan artifacts. We stopped at one case featuring a stone lion of an indeterminate age, timeless. It held me there with its presence; I could not move away. I waved the tour guide on and said I would catch up.

I felt the stone lion's story unwind as I stood there. The story was ancient, from long before the memory held by most of us in the present time. I stood in tears before this stone sculpture that had been weathered by centuries, had seen waves of generations. I did not quite understand my tears, except that I knew this lion was a powerful connection between the north and the south and represented knowledge that existed now in shards of memory and cultural practice. The lion showed me how it had been an important symbol of power as populations established themselves and grew, then declined as many departed in migrations. The lion's stone body, now porous from time and pollution, was exiled behind a glass cage. Hidden there, it carried a story important to many Native nations. It showed me how Pueblo peoples and Mvskoke peoples were linked in the long before. Our navel cord place had been marked by the lion, when it had stood in the place from which it had been taken.

I respectfully took out tobacco for a blessing for the lion. I remembered how there are sister stone lions in northern New Mexico. They are in the care of Pueblo peoples who know the details of their significance. There are lion or jaguar figures related to our Mvskoke people that are rooted in lands in the south, cared for by the indigenous peoples there.

There were many other powerful items in that museum, as there are in museums and universities all over the world. They carry power that belongs to certain places and peoples. They might be sad and lonely. Some can hear them cry out. They can cause unrest until they find their way home. They can bring peace, bring communities together when they are returned, celebrated, then laid to rest.

Everything leaves tracks, an energetic story trail of its presence, its story.

49 Dark Night

One day you notice you feel stuck in what feels like a kind of doldrum where there are no clearing winds of fresh thoughts. There is no way in or out.

This kind of period has been called "dark night of the soul" by the Spanish mystic and poet St. John of the Cross. It's a period of purification by trial.

I found myself there in a time when I had been dealing with losses of family members, by death or betrayal, and was lost in the grief of history. I began reviewing the path of my life and trying to figure out the direction forward. I knew I had to make friends with my own death. It is certain for every one of us.

When you get to my age, you either make an ally of death, or you run scared. I don't sense that I'm going any-time soon; there's still too much left for me to do. Yet, death is ever present. It's an essential part of life in this realm. Other realms have different laws. As with any difficulty, I go out by the river or into the trees to find a place for my soul to rest. I turn to the story with gratitude, for the spiritual illumination that can be found as the tale of the living continues to unwind.

It occurred to me that even this country and this being of time we occupy is also in a dark night of the soul, with the question being, will we choose compassionate ideas and laws, and leaders who serve and are fit for the job, or will we choose dictatorial pawns who assume authority for self-gain, and wish to oppress and police citizens to enslave them to a false story.

This earth too is also in the place of challenge and shift, another level of the dark night of the soul. Will there still be trees and rivers when we are through with our buying and selling?

I turned eastward to begin the day and take in breath. I gave it back with prayer for my family, even those who mean to harm, knowing that we are all family: these lands, these communities, this earth. I turned back to tend the story with the words, images, and music I have been given and knew that even the hardest parts of loss and heartbreak are what shines the soul and opens the door to understanding, to love.

50 *Illumination*

I want to give you this as it was given to me. Gifts of inspiration often come when we don't expect it, when we need it. I was in deep grief. And as I have been taught by those who have gone before, I walked east to greet the morning, to give thanks, to send prayer:

I was surprised by how in that dawn the light was everywhere, winding through the grasses, illuminating the trees, river, and the circling black and red birds who thought I was a flower in my yellow shirt. The light saturated the sky, my soul, everything. The Creator was a song moving through us. I heard it. We are a song! It was so tenderly beautiful I almost couldn't stand it. How will I ever sing it, speak it, be it?

51 *Gratitude Prayer*

We give thanks for you, the generations coming up behind us, as we drive east, home from one of the largest Native arts gatherings in Indian Country.

As we pass those piñon-filled hills, climb past the mountainous ridges that open to high desert plains, as the blue sky grows bluer than was even possible to imagine, as the clouds walk freely in the sky toward a meeting to make rain, as we cross over arroyos then rivers, as we make the miles over flatlands marked by wind farms and cattle, we give thanks for your presence, your art, your bravery, your music, and how you made it here to this place of celebration despite the challenges you face to find your way to the circle.

As we cross the border to our home state, as we drive up to our little red house next to the river on our reservation, as we unpack the saxophone and equipment needed to perform music with my favorite on-call band of musicians, as we carry all the bags inside under a sky so brilliant with stars the dark might sing, as we write down the mileage and lock up the van, as we unpack and shower, as we lay down our bodies weary with travel, we give thanks for the journey, that we made it home, that you made it or will make it home, we give thanks for every one of you who gathered together to celebrate the dream-making by the artists calling the next generations into the circle.

We give thanks as we continue to follow one day after another, as one night becomes day and day becomes night, and one year becomes two, then three, as there are children, grandchildren, then great-grandchildren, and though we might appear to falter, and the circle may appear to be broken, we continue in a spiral, in circle after circle of gratitude for the story and how, though it falters, we continue together in a spiral, circle after circle after circle, because we are compelled by love and beyond love—

We acknowledge you. We love you. We give thanks for this gift of life. We give thanks for you.

With gratitude, this prayer—

Acknowledgments

TRANSFORM

"Sunrise" from Joy Harjo, *Conflict Resolution for Holy Beings* (New York: W. W. Norton, 2015).

COMING OF AGE

Source material from Jean Chaudhuri and Joyotpaul Chaudhuri, *A Sacred Path: The Way of the Muscogee Creeks* (Los Angeles: UCLA American Indian Studies Center, 2001).

Excerpt from Joy Harjo, *For a Girl Becoming*, illustrated by Mercedes McDonald (Tucson: University of Arizona Press, 2009) and Joy Harjo, *For a Girl Becoming*, illustrated by Adriana Garcia (New York: Norton Young Readers, 2025).

These stories would not exist without teachers and mentors. Most of my cultural and healing mentors have passed on from this story realm. They include my great-aunt Lois Harjo Ball; cousins George Coser Sr. and George Coser Jr; Reggie Arthur, Karen Leialoha Carroll; Barbara Matayoshi; Alva Andrews; Tim Thompson; Robert Brown; and my uncle John Pershing Jacobs. Some would not want to be named, and I respect their wishes. Others I found in poetry, literature, music, and the arts are too numerous to be named. They know who they are, and I honor them as I continue through this discipline of living. They are in my words, my thoughts, my music.

I continue to be grateful for my faithful editor at W. W. Norton, Jill Bialosky. She has been beside me almost since the beginning of this publishing life. And gratitude for Anya Backlund, who sees to all the travel and events. I could have no better ally. And to Jin Auh, my special agent on the road of permissions and publishing. A special note here for copyeditor Janet McDonald, whose skill and care is evident throughout this manuscript. And I appreciate Laura Mucha, editorial assistant, who has accompanied this book patiently to publication. And *mvto* to Jennifer Foerster, my brilliant assistant and a fine poet who helps with all the messages, editing, and details. For my husband, Owen Sapulpa, who inspires me to be curious, to reach beyond knowing. He and his family brought love without measure into my life. And for my circle of friends and family who are ever generous with their love.